SCHEHERAZADE'S CAT

Other Tuttle books
by Amy Zerner and Jessie Spicer Zerner:

Zen ABC

The Dream Quilt
(forthcoming)

SCHEHERAZADE'S CAT

& Other Fables
from Around the World

RETOLD AND ILLUSTRATED BY
AMY ZERNER & JESSIE SPICER ZERNER

CHARLES E. TUTTLE COMPANY, INC.
Boston   •   Rutland, Vermont   •   Tokyo

With love and appreciation to Monte Farber,
our magical hero and mighty defender,
and to Kit-Kat, the calico muse

CHARLES E. TUTTLE COMPANY, INC.
of Rutland, Vermont and Tokyo Japan
with editorial offices at
77 Central Street, Boston, Massachusetts 02109

ISBN 0-8048-1807-X
Library of Congress CIP data is available for this title.

First Edition
1 3 5 7 9 10 8 6 4 2

PRINTED IN SINGAPORE

CONTENTS

SCHEHERAZADE'S CAT

Arabia

*I*t happened one day in a walled garden of an elegant Arabian house that a cat called Kalico raised her head from a nap and flicked her ears toward a nightingale who was singing a sad story. Kalico's dreams of fish and catnip had been interrupted by this winged visitor from the world outside.

"Not again!" she thought as the words became clear. "Soon there will be no maiden left in this kingdom. All the mothers and fathers have sent their daughters away. Next it will be Scheherazade, my darling mistress. Then who will smooth my fur and feed me food from her very own plate?"

She shook her head in disbelief and scratched her jeweled collar, but no warning bell rang—Kalico was a friend to all the birds. How boring life would be without their melodic tales. Even mice, held firmly under her furry paw, would gaze into her great green eyes and speak of dragons and princesses and distant lands where cats were gods. No cats ever visited the garden, however, for there were none left. They had all been banished from this kingdom by its irate ruler.

The King's first wife, it was said, has run off with a handsome sailor lad. She had grown tired of being waited upon hand and foot, tired of the beautiful palace where her every wish was granted, and tired of her husband whose only desire was to make her happy. Indeed, she was a good deal like her cat, Hakim, a large, ginger-colored fellow who lived only for the moment and was left behind when the Queen departed for a life of adventure.

When the King discovered his wife's treachery, he grabbed Hakim and shook him until his earrings flew off and his whiskers were bent. Hakim, as any spirited, spoiled cat would, scratched his majesty severely on the nose. From then on, cats were forbidden in that country by law. Even worse, the King could neither trust nor love any woman again. He decided in anger, and with his terrible power, that he would take wives but would allow them to remain only one night. When the sun rose, they would be killed. In this way, no wife could again betray him!

And this was the nightingale's lament. The King was once more looking for a queen. His adviser, the vizier and Scheherazade's father, had been sent to search for an acceptable girl and had found no one.

"No one," the nightingale sang mournfully in his lonely voice, "no one except—"

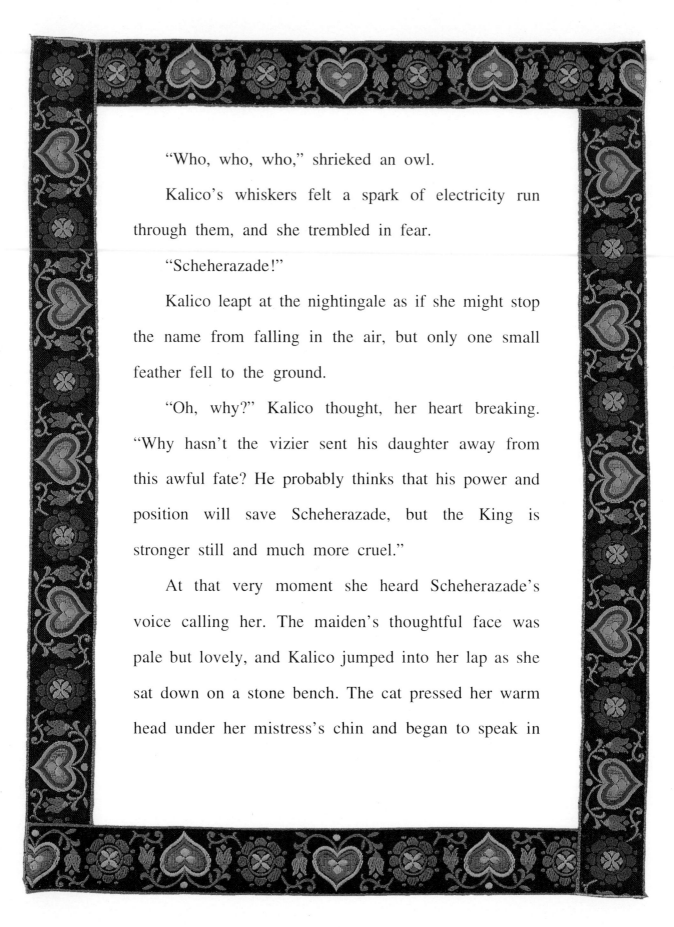

"Who, who, who," shrieked an owl.

Kalico's whiskers felt a spark of electricity run through them, and she trembled in fear.

"Scheherazade!"

Kalico leapt at the nightingale as if she might stop the name from falling in the air, but only one small feather fell to the ground.

"Oh, why?" Kalico thought, her heart breaking. "Why hasn't the vizier sent his daughter away from this awful fate? He probably thinks that his power and position will save Scheherazade, but the King is stronger still and much more cruel."

At that very moment she heard Scheherazade's voice calling her. The maiden's thoughtful face was pale but lovely, and Kalico jumped into her lap as she sat down on a stone bench. The cat pressed her warm head under her mistress's chin and began to speak in tiny growls, purrs, and murmurs. They shared a special language and understood each other perfectly.

Scheherazade's anxious eyes roamed over the garden as Kalico tried to comfort her. The girl listened and thought until her eyes fell upon a pile of books left forgotten beside a rosebush. Kalico's eyes followed those of her mistress, and as she saw the books, she held her breath for a moment. An idea had come to her.

"What makes time pass more quickly than a story?" Kalico thought. "How long and dull the day would be without the tales of the birds and others who visit this garden." She shut her eyes in deep concentration and then opened them wide in a green blaze of excitement.

"I know the answer, dear Scheherazade," she purred. "Here is a plan." Her pink mouth drew close to

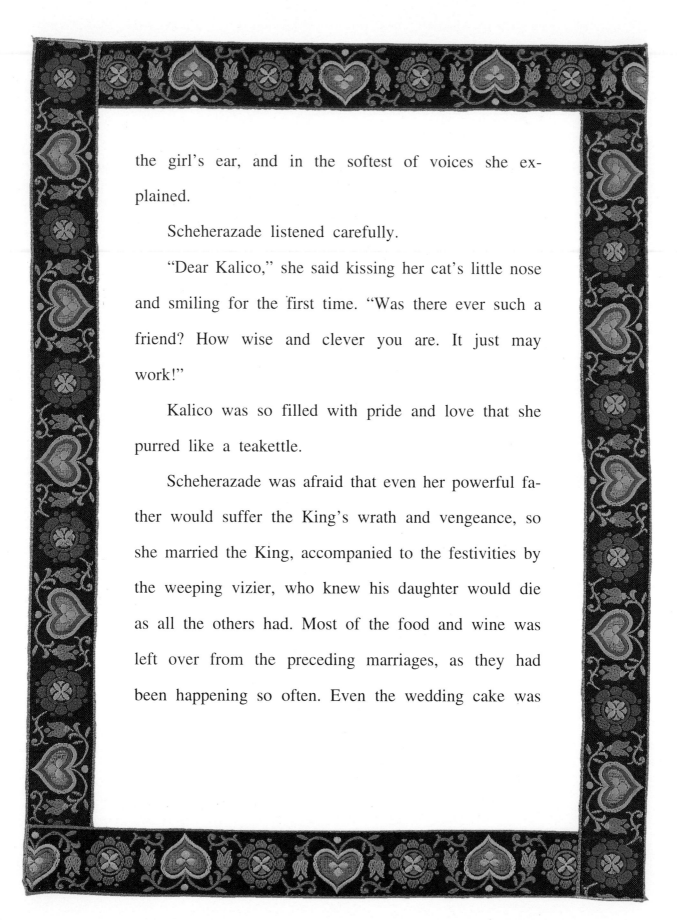

the girl's ear, and in the softest of voices she explained.

Scheherazade listened carefully.

"Dear Kalico," she said kissing her cat's little nose and smiling for the first time. "Was there ever such a friend? How wise and clever you are. It just may work!"

Kalico was so filled with pride and love that she purred like a teakettle.

Scheherazade was afraid that even her powerful father would suffer the King's wrath and vengeance, so she married the King, accompanied to the festivities by the weeping vizier, who knew his daughter would die as all the others had. Most of the food and wine was left over from the preceding marriages, as they had been happening so often. Even the wedding cake was stale, for no one seemed to have much appetite at these affairs anymore.

When the guests had sadly departed, the first evening stars were appearing in the sky.

"Let us retire," said the King, who was quite sleepy from all the wine he had drunk. They entered the royal chambers, and the moon made a shining path across the floor. In the distance, a nightingale sang faintly. Perhaps he was telling Kalico of the day's events, Scheherazade thought, and suddenly felt reassured.

"My lord," she said in her charming voice, "I have a fancy to tell you a bedtime story. Ever since childhood, such tales have been dear to me. It will lift the cares of the day from you, excellent sir, and ease your way into a happy sleep."

The King was surprised at such thoughtfulness. He

suspected nothing, and had already given his guards the orders to kill Scheherazade the moment the sun came up.

Scheherazade was a born storyteller. Her words painted pictures and the plot had as many twists and turns as a ball of wool in a paws of a cat. The King remained wide awake and was so interested in the tale that he did not realize how quickly the time had passed. The first pale pink rays of the sun shone through the arched windows and with them appeared the grim, armed guards, prepared to do their horrible duty. The startled King awoke abruptly from the enchanted dream-web that Scheherazade had woven about him with her story. He remembered the cruel orders he had given to be carried out at dawn. Scheherazade's heart trembled at that moment but she showed no outward fear. Before the swords could be drawn and her life ended, the King leapt to his feet and stood, hand raised to protect her. He then waved his men away.

"But you have not finished this wonderful story," the King said.

Scheherazade yawned delicately and rubbed her eyes. "But I am too exhausted now. Tonight, my lord, we shall continue, and you shall hear the exciting ending to this tale."

The King, too, was ready for a nap and much too intrigued not to allow Scheherazade to finish her story. And so she did, that clever girl, and for many nights after that, always found herself just in the middle of a story when the sun rose. For this had been Kalico's plan. That wise cat who so loved to listen to the birds had thought of this wonderful way to save her mistress's life, and every evening the nightingale carried the good news of Scheherazade's success back to Kalico's garden.

Hundreds of stories were recounted, until Scheherazade began to fear that her seemingly endless store of entertainment might come to an end. She searched endlessly through her books until it seem that there were only three or four new stories left to tell. Her face grew pale and drawn, and she begged to return to her garden for just one day to rest and refresh herself.

Kalico was so happy to see her that her purrs filled the garden with a happy sound.

"Oh, dearest Kalico," cried Scheherazade, snuggling her cat. "You have saved me for many a day, but my time is running out."

Kalico listened quietly. The cat's green eyes were filled with mystery and wisdom. It was not long before her mistress felt her spirits lift, and a smile of delight warmed her face, for Kalico had thought of another plan. It was, as all good plans are, very simple, and Scheherazade was sure it would work.

A few nights later, Scheherazade wore her usual long, flowing garments, and unseen beneath her veil, except for a whisker or the tip of a tail, she carried Kalico. The King asked for his usual bedtime story and stroked his wife's hair kindly when she began to speak in her sweet low voice. As the night progressed, she paused occasionally and seemed to be interrupted by a faint mewing sound. The sleepy King never noticed, and morning found her safe once again.

For one thousand and one nights, Scheherazade told her stories without fear or lack of inspiration. The King was so entranced that he forgot completely that he had once wished her dead. He became a different

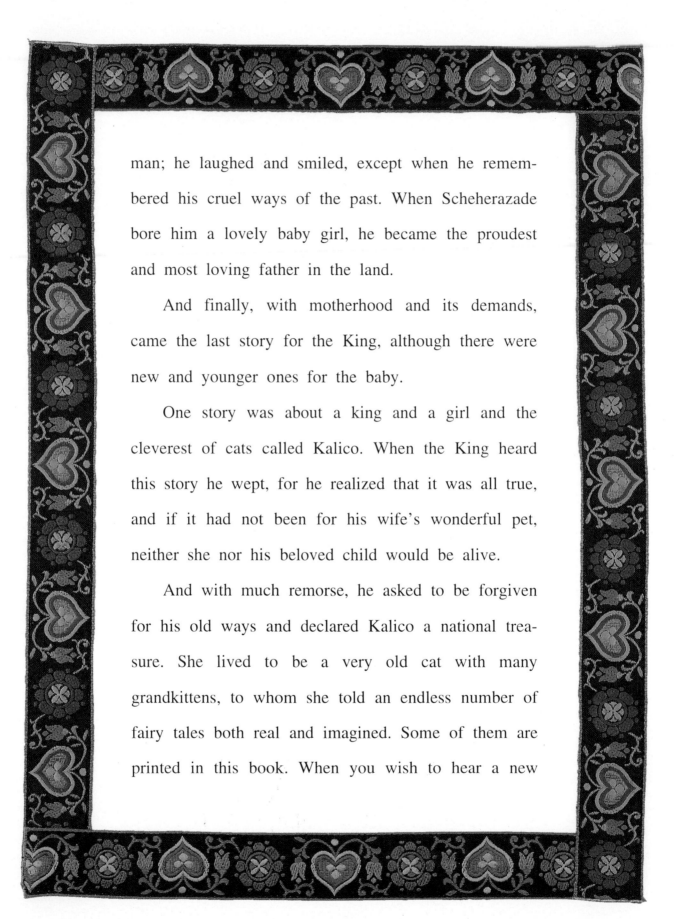

man; he laughed and smiled, except when he remembered his cruel ways of the past. When Scheherazade bore him a lovely baby girl, he became the proudest and most loving father in the land.

And finally, with motherhood and its demands, came the last story for the King, although there were new and younger ones for the baby.

One story was about a king and a girl and the cleverest of cats called Kalico. When the King heard this story he wept, for he realized that it was all true, and if it had not been for his wife's wonderful pet, neither she nor his beloved child would be alive.

And with much remorse, he asked to be forgiven for his old ways and declared Kalico a national treasure. She lived to be a very old cat with many grandkittens, to whom she told an endless number of fairy tales both real and imagined. Some of them are printed in this book. When you wish to hear a new story, Kalico herself would be the first to tell you: "Just listen to the nightingale when the first stars of the evening light the sky."

THE JEWELED
FROG

Peru

By a quiet pool, at the side of a cloud-topped mountain in Peru, lived a small green frog and his large green family. When the early evenings darkened the sky, the frogs would gather on the slippery banks by the water and listen to family legends and to stories of the land that lay beyond their tranquil home. The little frog was the youngest of many brothers and sisters, and his life seemed very ordinary when he heard of his relatives' wild adventures.

"Sometimes the sun was so large and hot that it sucked the water from the ground," his green grandfather croaked. "Your toes turned brown and you could hardly hop across the hot earth."

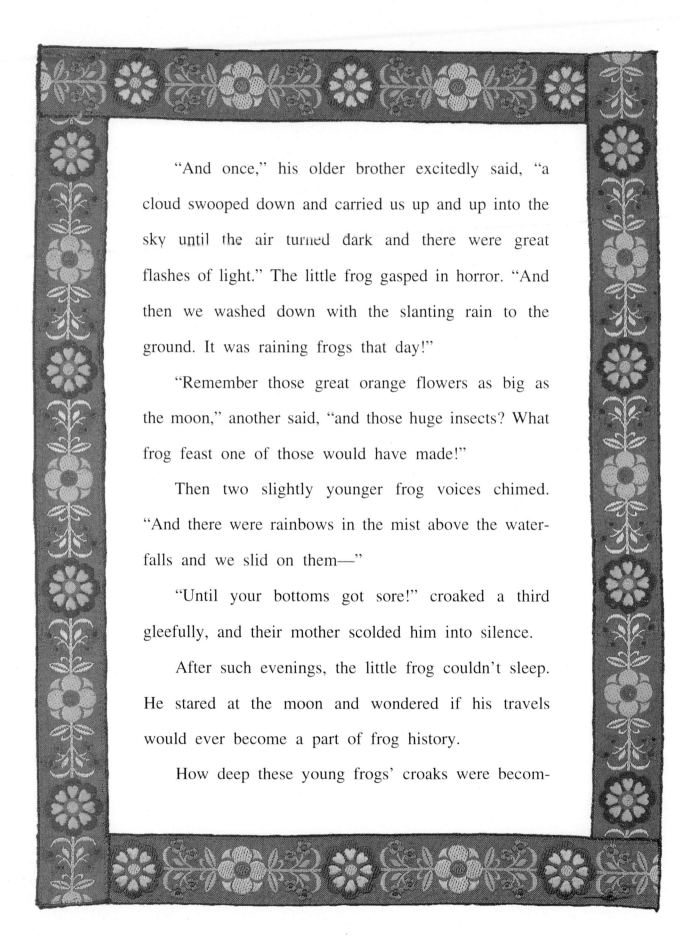

"And once," his older brother excitedly said, "a cloud swooped down and carried us up and up into the sky until the air turned dark and there were great flashes of light." The little frog gasped in horror. "And then we washed down with the slanting rain to the ground. It was raining frogs that day!"

"Remember those great orange flowers as big as the moon," another said, "and those huge insects? What frog feast one of those would have made!"

Then two slightly younger frog voices chimed. "And there were rainbows in the mist above the waterfalls and we slid on them—"

"Until your bottoms got sore!" croaked a third gleefully, and their mother scolded him into silence.

After such evenings, the little frog couldn't sleep. He stared at the moon and wondered if his travels would ever become a part of frog history.

How deep these young frogs' croaks were becom-

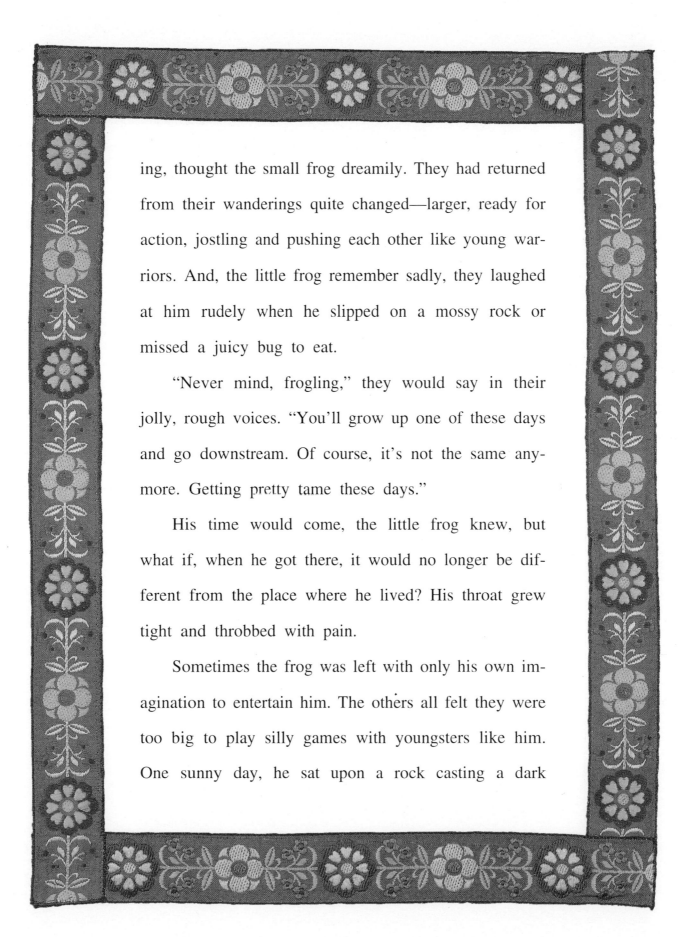

ing, thought the small frog dreamily. They had returned from their wanderings quite changed—larger, ready for action, jostling and pushing each other like young warriors. And, the little frog remember sadly, they laughed at him rudely when he slipped on a mossy rock or missed a juicy bug to eat.

"Never mind, frogling," they would say in their jolly, rough voices. "You'll grow up one of these days and go downstream. Of course, it's not the same anymore. Getting pretty tame these days."

His time would come, the little frog knew, but what if, when he got there, it would no longer be different from the place where he lived? His throat grew tight and throbbed with pain.

Sometimes the frog was left with only his own imagination to entertain him. The others all felt they were too big to play silly games with youngsters like him. One sunny day, he sat upon a rock casting a dark shadow, as dark as his thoughts, until, as he stretched his legs, he saw the shadow change and change again with every move he made. Curving his back and holding up two toes, his shadow became a horned snail. Standing tall on two hind feet, he became a giant frog, and using a lily flower as a trumpet, he screamed into the rocks until his voice sounded like thunder. Several of his sisters splashed madly in the water at the noise, and the little frog laughed raucously until they pelted him with small stones. It was magical! Life was already exciting. Except on cloudy days, of course, when he slept under the green leaves and dreamed away the long afternoons.

Once in a while, as the small green frog sat upon the rock amusing himself, he would see a young girl coming down the steep mountain path carrying a load of wash to the stream. Always hovering behind her was a monstrous, bloody-beaked bird. Bald and hunchbacked, with a ruff of unkempt feathers about his scrawny neck, the king condor was a frightening sight. The frog would quickly hide in the water when they approached and peep out from the rock's deep shadow. A king condor was certainly to be feared, and this one was larger than all the other condors, ruling his domain by terror. His great talons extended, he would plunge downward through the sky to grasp his victims and carry them away to his mountain cave where they became his dinner or, as in the young girl's case, his slaves.

The condor ordered the girl about, mocking her tears of sadness and her longing for her parents.

"They have forgotten you," he sneered. "You are better off here. At least there is plenty of good, red meat to eat.

Every day the little frog found himself listening to their conversations with more and more interest.

Collyur, or "morning star," was the girl's name.

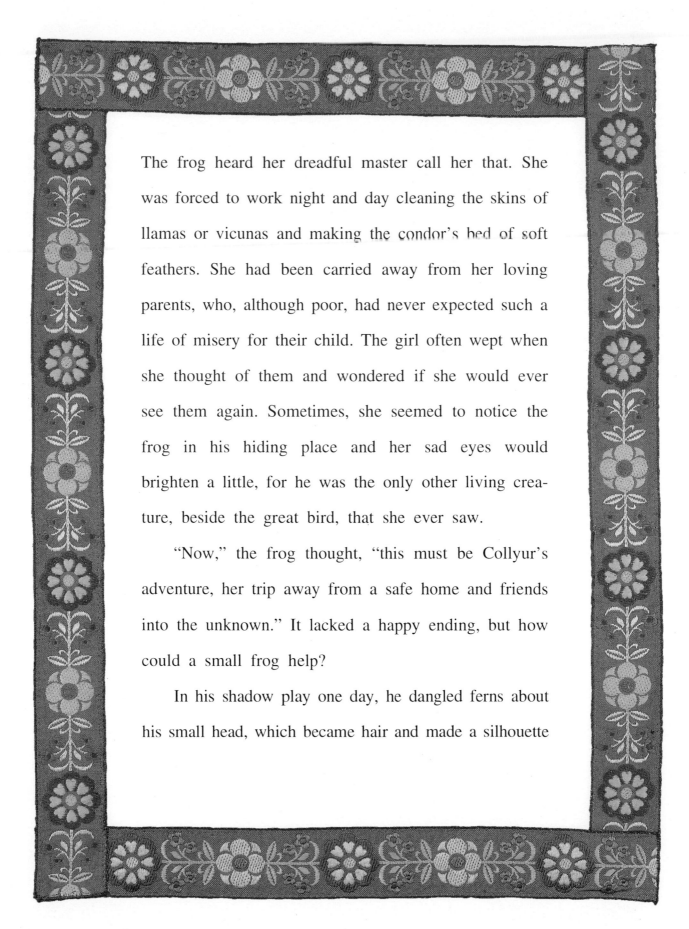

The frog heard her dreadful master call her that. She was forced to work night and day cleaning the skins of llamas or vicunas and making the condor's bed of soft feathers. She had been carried away from her loving parents, who, although poor, had never expected such a life of misery for their child. The girl often wept when she thought of them and wondered if she would ever see them again. Sometimes, she seemed to notice the frog in his hiding place and her sad eyes would brighten a little, for he was the only other living creature, beside the great bird, that she ever saw.

"Now," the frog thought, "this must be Collyur's adventure, her trip away from a safe home and friends into the unknown." It lacked a happy ending, but how could a small frog help?

In his shadow play one day, he dangled ferns about his small head, which became hair and made a silhouette

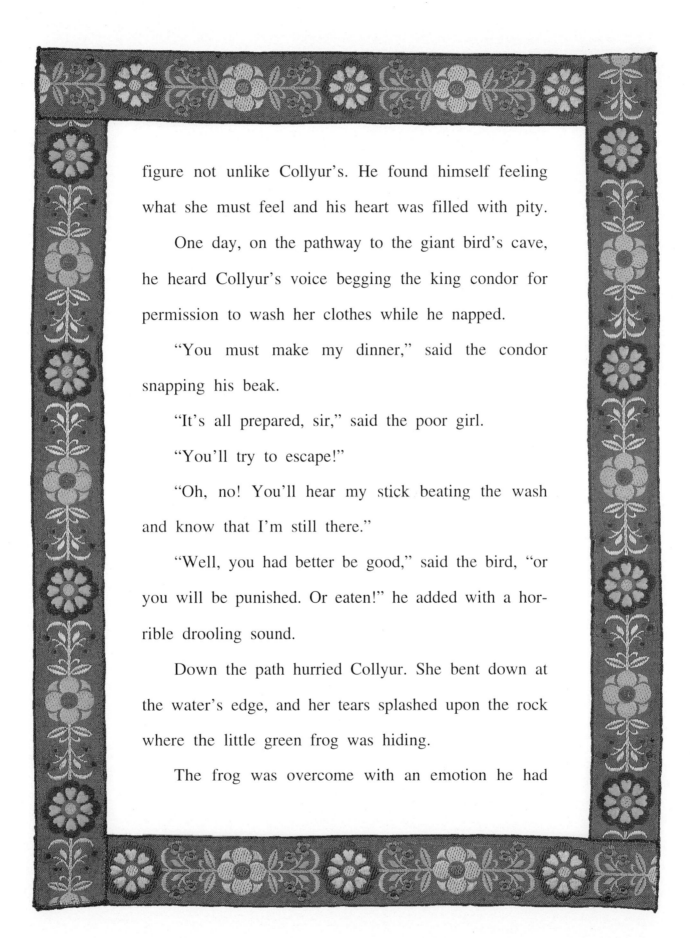

figure not unlike Collyur's. He found himself feeling what she must feel and his heart was filled with pity.

One day, on the pathway to the giant bird's cave, he heard Collyur's voice begging the king condor for permission to wash her clothes while he napped.

"You must make my dinner," said the condor snapping his beak.

"It's all prepared, sir," said the poor girl.

"You'll try to escape!"

"Oh, no! You'll hear my stick beating the wash and know that I'm still there."

"Well, you had better be good," said the bird, "or you will be punished. Or eaten!" he added with a horrible drooling sound.

Down the path hurried Collyur. She bent down at the water's edge, and her tears splashed upon the rock where the little green frog was hiding.

The frog was overcome with an emotion he had

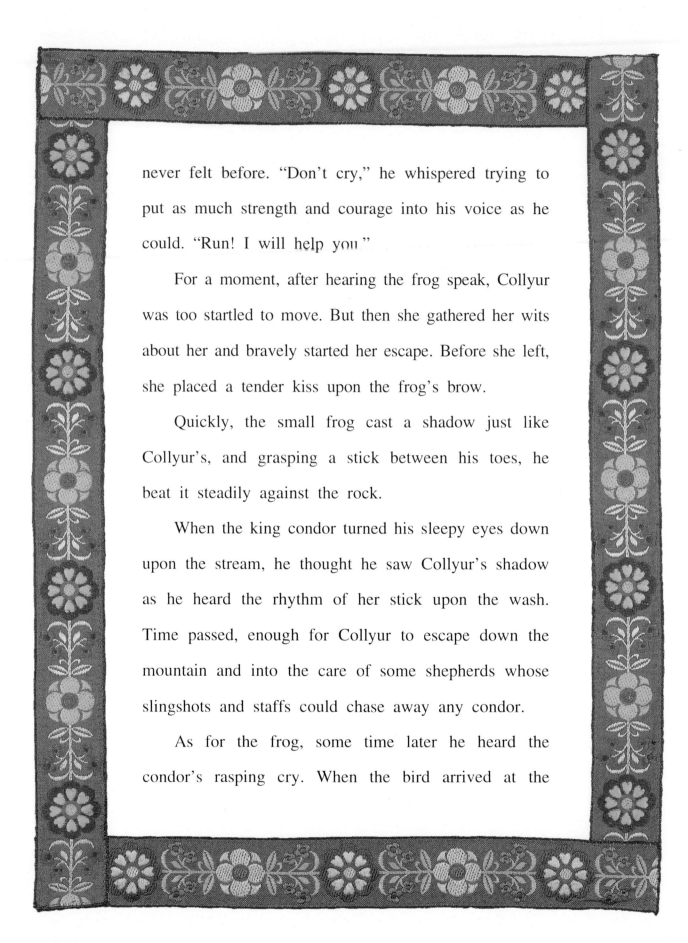

never felt before. "Don't cry," he whispered trying to put as much strength and courage into his voice as he could. "Run! I will help you."

For a moment, after hearing the frog speak, Collyur was too startled to move. But then she gathered her wits about her and bravely started her escape. Before she left, she placed a tender kiss upon the frog's brow.

Quickly, the small frog cast a shadow just like Collyur's, and grasping a stick between his toes, he beat it steadily against the rock.

When the king condor turned his sleepy eyes down upon the stream, he thought he saw Collyur's shadow as he heard the rhythm of her stick upon the wash. Time passed, enough for Collyur to escape down the mountain and into the care of some shepherds whose slingshots and staffs could chase away any condor.

As for the frog, some time later he heard the condor's rasping cry. When the bird arrived at the stream, he saw nothing but a small splash and a pile of clothes.

The little frog swam slowly home. He felt brave and confident and realized for the first time that adventure was everywhere. It could happen to anyone; small or large, young or old, it made no difference. Suddenly, in a moment, an entire life could be changed. The frog shouted in happiness when he saw his large, green family sitting on the slippery bank in the early evening. As he looked into their faces, he noticed that something had happened to him. Glancing down into the water, he saw with amazement a beautiful star-shaped jewel shining like the morning star where Collyur had kissed him.

Indeed, the star was a medal for bravery and was worn by all of the frog's descendants to remind them that wonderful things can happen to small green frogs with large imaginations.

THE WISHING BIRD

South Africa

Long before our great-great-grandfathers were born, a boy called Duma lived in the southern part of Africa. Sometimes his parents, who were poor farmers, left Duma at home while they went to tend their field when the weather was hot. And this was just such a day.

"There's some cold porridge on the table for lunch," called his mother as she and his father left for work, their hoes over their shoulders. "We'll be back before dark."

"And don't bother the goat," shouted his father as they rounded the dusty curve of the road. "It's much too hot and she should stay quiet in the shade."

Duma watched the little dust clouds fly up, and his mind felt as empty as the road. Then he went into the hut and ate the porridge while watching a black spider with yellow dots weave a web in the corner of the window.

"How do you do that?" asked Duma curiously. The spider said nothing, as it was eating a plump fly with great enjoyment.

"Aha," said Duma, "it's a bug trap."

One thing lead to another, and Duma unraveled a piece of his mother's fine weaving. It was filled with colors, and he thought it would make a splendid web. He could be a spider too.

For several hours, he tirelessly strung the thread between two small trees. It was rather messy, he thought, as he stepped back to admire it, but surely a bug wouldn't notice.

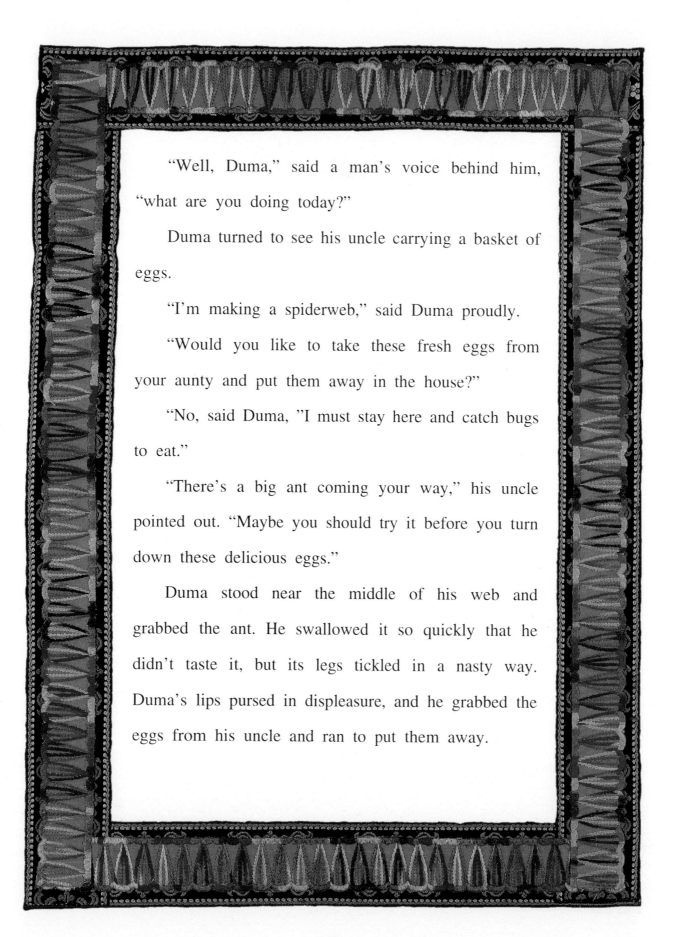

"Well, Duma," said a man's voice behind him, "what are you doing today?"

Duma turned to see his uncle carrying a basket of eggs.

"I'm making a spiderweb," said Duma proudly.

"Would you like to take these fresh eggs from your aunty and put them away in the house?"

"No, said Duma, "I must stay here and catch bugs to eat."

"There's a big ant coming your way," his uncle pointed out. "Maybe you should try it before you turn down these delicious eggs."

Duma stood near the middle of his web and grabbed the ant. He swallowed it so quickly that he didn't taste it, but its legs tickled in a nasty way. Duma's lips pursed in displeasure, and he grabbed the eggs from his uncle and ran to put them away.

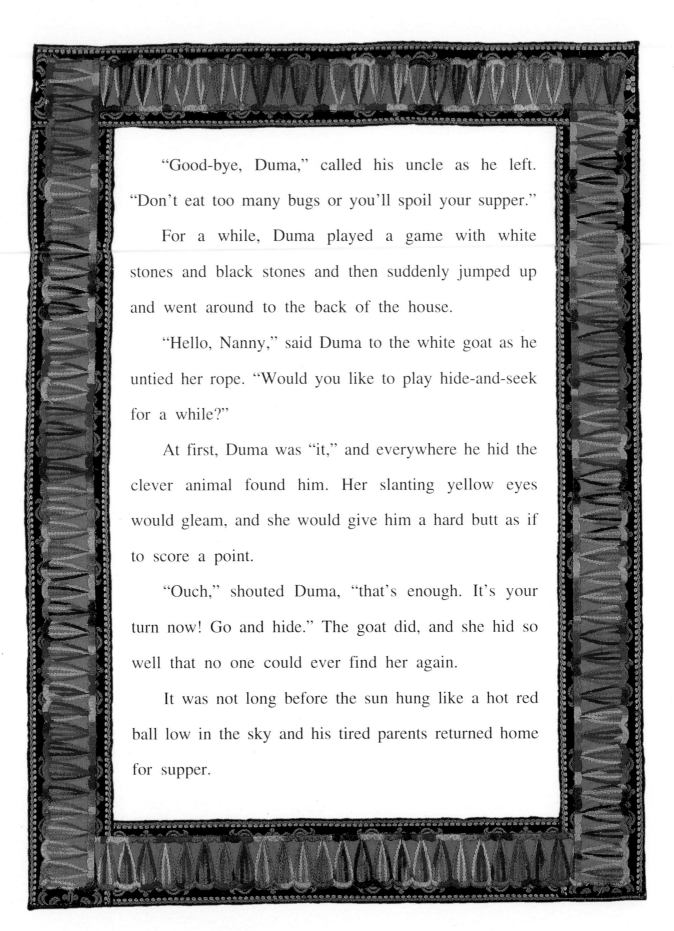

"Good-bye, Duma," called his uncle as he left. "Don't eat too many bugs or you'll spoil your supper."

For a while, Duma played a game with white stones and black stones and then suddenly jumped up and went around to the back of the house.

"Hello, Nanny," said Duma to the white goat as he untied her rope. "Would you like to play hide-and-seek for a while?"

At first, Duma was "it," and everywhere he hid the clever animal found him. Her slanting yellow eyes would gleam, and she would give him a hard butt as if to score a point.

"Ouch," shouted Duma, "that's enough. It's your turn now! Go and hide." The goat did, and she hid so well that no one could ever find her again.

It was not long before the sun hung like a hot red ball low in the sky and his tired parents returned home for supper.

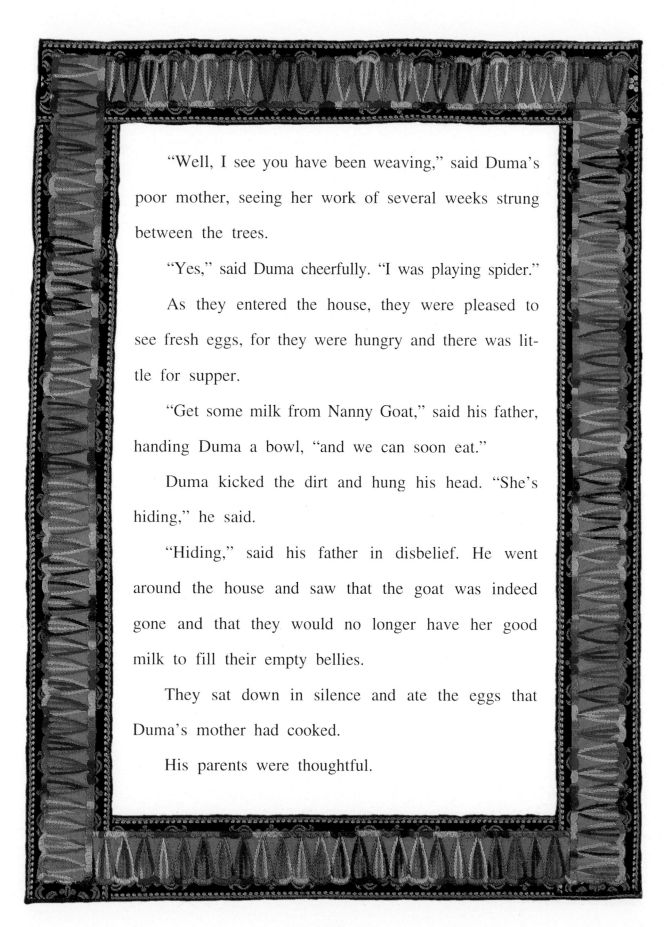

"Well, I see you have been weaving," said Duma's poor mother, seeing her work of several weeks strung between the trees.

"Yes," said Duma cheerfully. "I was playing spider."

As they entered the house, they were pleased to see fresh eggs, for they were hungry and there was little for supper.

"Get some milk from Nanny Goat," said his father, handing Duma a bowl, "and we can soon eat."

Duma kicked the dirt and hung his head. "She's hiding," he said.

"Hiding," said his father in disbelief. He went around the house and saw that the goat was indeed gone and that they would no longer have her good milk to fill their empty bellies.

They sat down in silence and ate the eggs that Duma's mother had cooked.

His parents were thoughtful.

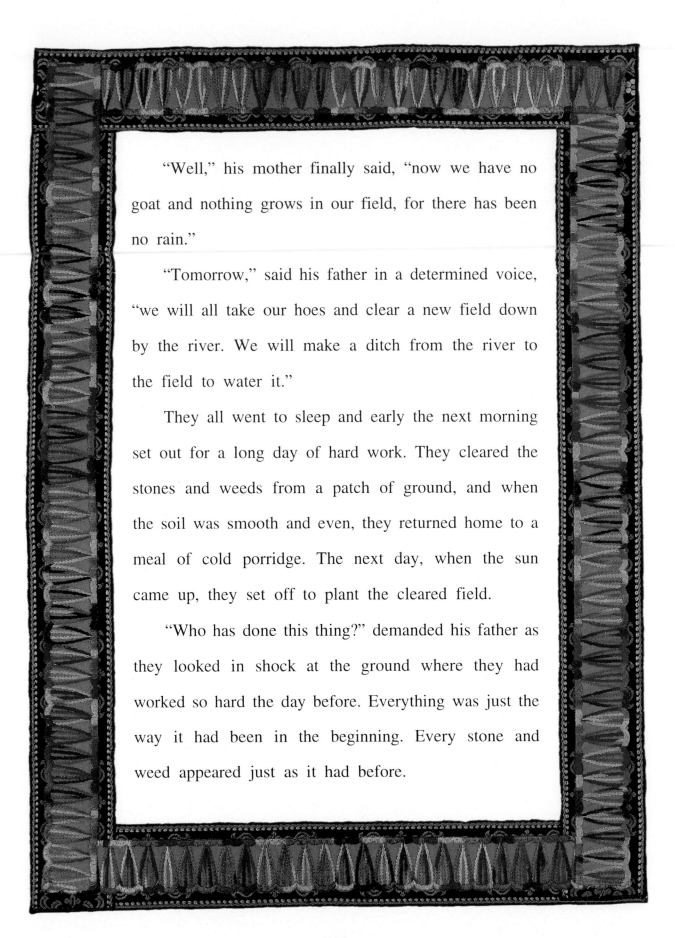

"Well," his mother finally said, "now we have no goat and nothing grows in our field, for there has been no rain."

"Tomorrow," said his father in a determined voice, "we will all take our hoes and clear a new field down by the river. We will make a ditch from the river to the field to water it."

They all went to sleep and early the next morning set out for a long day of hard work. They cleared the stones and weeds from a patch of ground, and when the soil was smooth and even, they returned home to a meal of cold porridge. The next day, when the sun came up, they set off to plant the cleared field.

"Who has done this thing?" demanded his father as they looked in shock at the ground where they had worked so hard the day before. Everything was just the way it had been in the beginning. Every stone and weed appeared just as it had before.

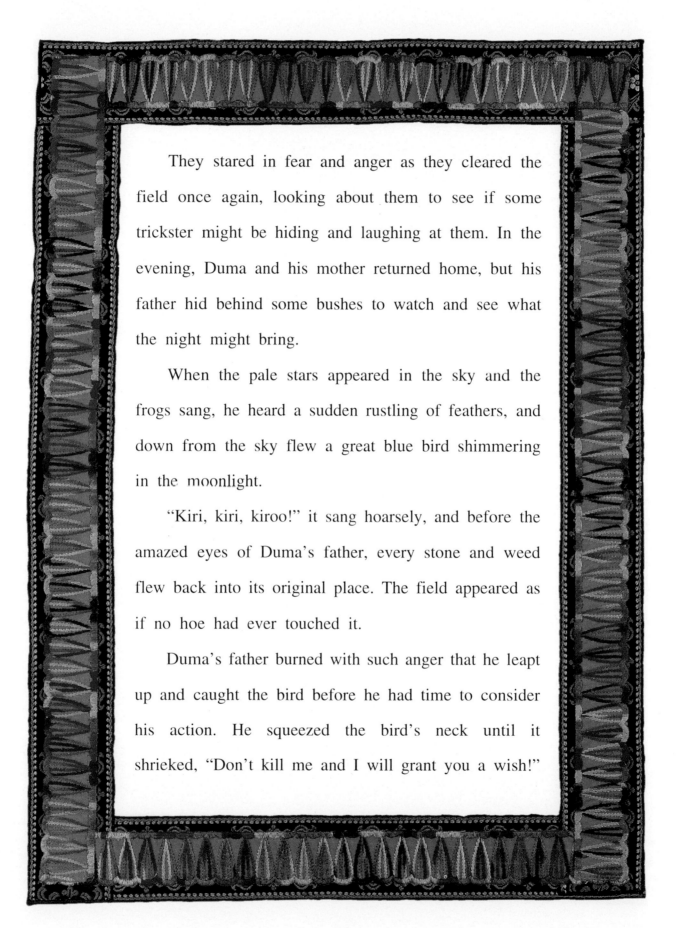

They stared in fear and anger as they cleared the field once again, looking about them to see if some trickster might be hiding and laughing at them. In the evening, Duma and his mother returned home, but his father hid behind some bushes to watch and see what the night might bring.

When the pale stars appeared in the sky and the frogs sang, he heard a sudden rustling of feathers, and down from the sky flew a great blue bird shimmering in the moonlight.

"Kiri, kiri, kiroo!" it sang hoarsely, and before the amazed eyes of Duma's father, every stone and weed flew back into its original place. The field appeared as if no hoe had ever touched it.

Duma's father burned with such anger that he leapt up and caught the bird before he had time to consider his action. He squeezed the bird's neck until it shrieked, "Don't kill me and I will grant you a wish!"

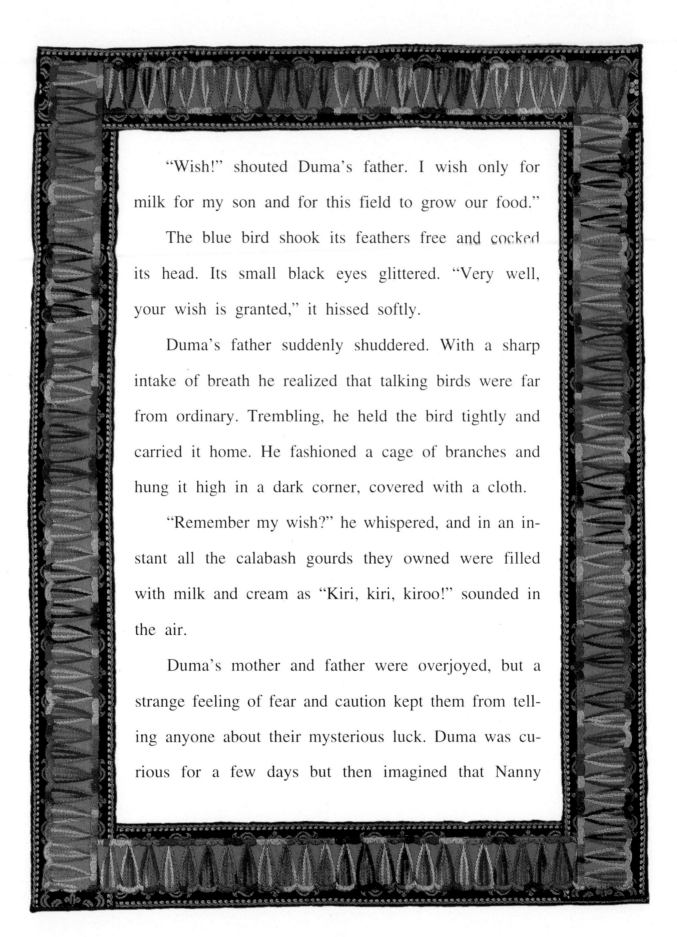

"Wish!" shouted Duma's father. I wish only for milk for my son and for this field to grow our food."

The blue bird shook its feathers free and cocked its head. Its small black eyes glittered. "Very well, your wish is granted," it hissed softly.

Duma's father suddenly shuddered. With a sharp intake of breath he realized that talking birds were far from ordinary. Trembling, he held the bird tightly and carried it home. He fashioned a cage of branches and hung it high in a dark corner, covered with a cloth.

"Remember my wish?" he whispered, and in an instant all the calabash gourds they owned were filled with milk and cream as "Kiri, kiri, kiroo!" sounded in the air.

Duma's mother and father were overjoyed, but a strange feeling of fear and caution kept them from telling anyone about their mysterious luck. Duma was curious for a few days but then imagined that Nanny

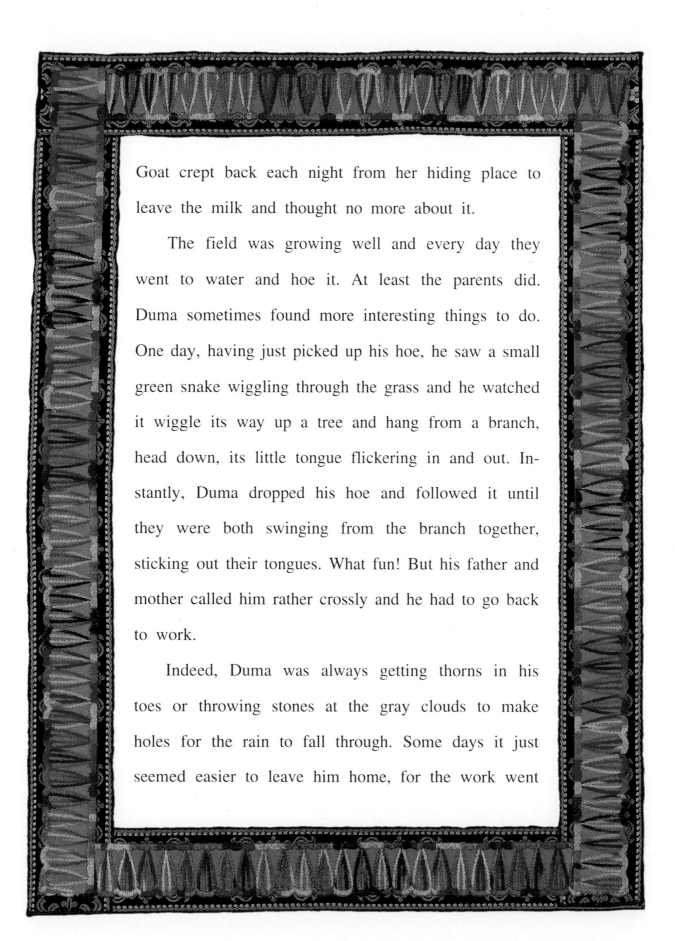

Goat crept back each night from her hiding place to leave the milk and thought no more about it.

The field was growing well and every day they went to water and hoe it. At least the parents did. Duma sometimes found more interesting things to do. One day, having just picked up his hoe, he saw a small green snake wiggling through the grass and he watched it wiggle its way up a tree and hang from a branch, head down, its little tongue flickering in and out. Instantly, Duma dropped his hoe and followed it until they were both swinging from the branch together, sticking out their tongues. What fun! But his father and mother called him rather crossly and he had to go back to work.

Indeed, Duma was always getting thorns in his toes or throwing stones at the gray clouds to make holes for the rain to fall through. Some days it just seemed easier to leave him home, for the work went

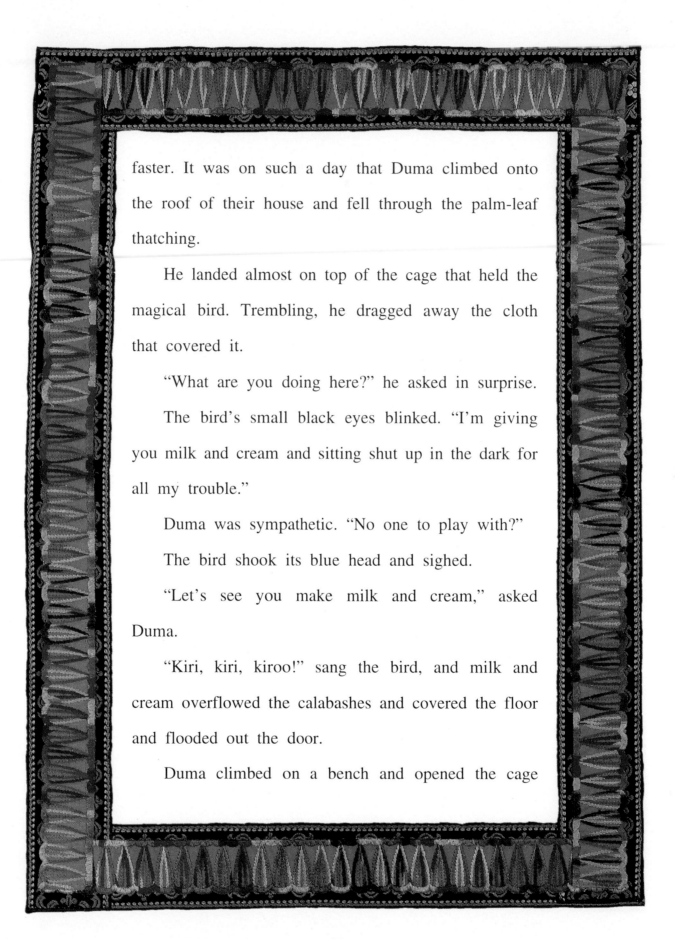

faster. It was on such a day that Duma climbed onto the roof of their house and fell through the palm-leaf thatching.

He landed almost on top of the cage that held the magical bird. Trembling, he dragged away the cloth that covered it.

"What are you doing here?" he asked in surprise.

The bird's small black eyes blinked. "I'm giving you milk and cream and sitting shut up in the dark for all my trouble."

Duma was sympathetic. "No one to play with?"

The bird shook its blue head and sighed.

"Let's see you make milk and cream," asked Duma.

"Kiri, kiri, kiroo!" sang the bird, and milk and cream overflowed the calabashes and covered the floor and flooded out the door.

Duma climbed on a bench and opened the cage

door. "Surely, that's enough milk and cream for a long, long time," he thought.

When his parents came home in the late afternoon, they found Duma sailing twig boats down a small river of milk and cream and an empty cage.

"You silly boy," they shouted, "now we will go hungry again. You must learn a lesson."

Duma was surprised to hear them saying such things and even more puzzled when they took him a long way from his hut and left him in the forest in a deep, rocky ravine. Of course, they planned to leave him there just long enough to frighten him and make him behave more responsibly.

Duma sat down on a rock for a while, and then it occurred to him that this was all a sort of game or trick. He would find his way home and they would all laugh together. It did not take him long to climb a tall tree and jump down on the other side of the ravine.

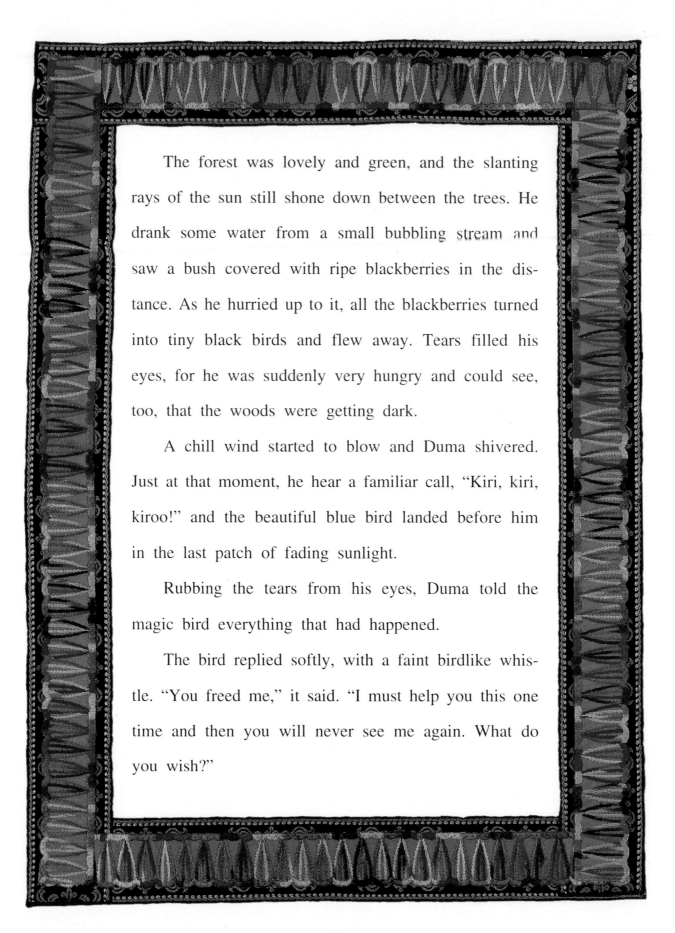

The forest was lovely and green, and the slanting rays of the sun still shone down between the trees. He drank some water from a small bubbling stream and saw a bush covered with ripe blackberries in the distance. As he hurried up to it, all the blackberries turned into tiny black birds and flew away. Tears filled his eyes, for he was suddenly very hungry and could see, too, that the woods were getting dark.

A chill wind started to blow and Duma shivered. Just at that moment, he hear a familiar call, "Kiri, kiri, kiroo!" and the beautiful blue bird landed before him in the last patch of fading sunlight.

Rubbing the tears from his eyes, Duma told the magic bird everything that had happened.

The bird replied softly, with a faint birdlike whistle. "You freed me," it said. "I must help you this one time and then you will never see me again. What do you wish?"

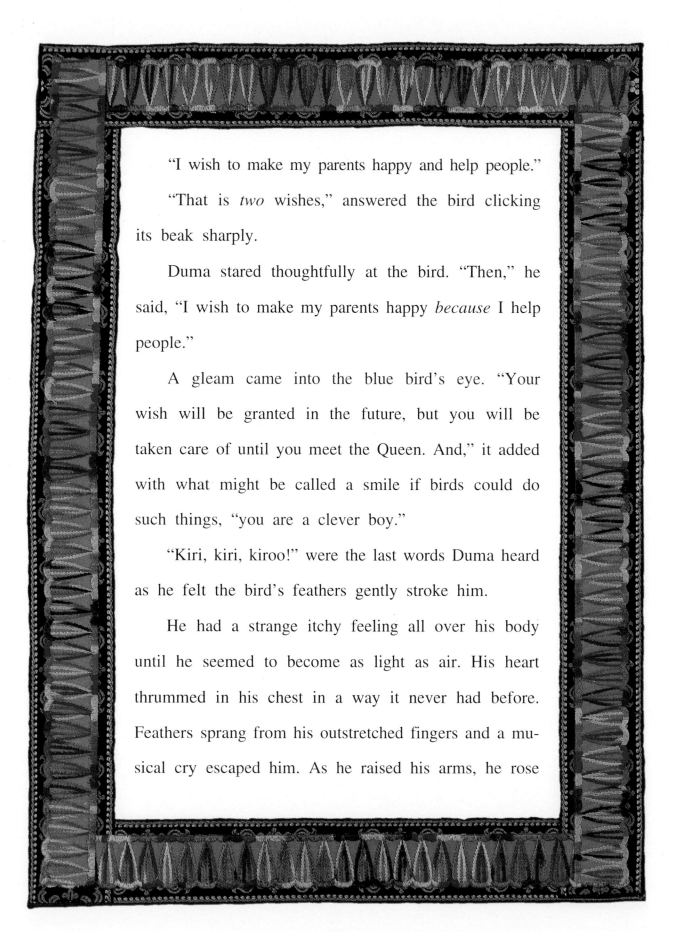

"I wish to make my parents happy and help people."

"That is *two* wishes," answered the bird clicking its beak sharply.

Duma stared thoughtfully at the bird. "Then," he said, "I wish to make my parents happy *because* I help people."

A gleam came into the blue bird's eye. "Your wish will be granted in the future, but you will be taken care of until you meet the Queen. And," it added with what might be called a smile if birds could do such things, "you are a clever boy."

"Kiri, kiri, kiroo!" were the last words Duma heard as he felt the bird's feathers gently stroke him.

He had a strange itchy feeling all over his body until he seemed to become as light as air. His heart thrummed in his chest in a way it never had before. Feathers sprang from his outstretched fingers and a musical cry escaped him. As he raised his arms, he rose

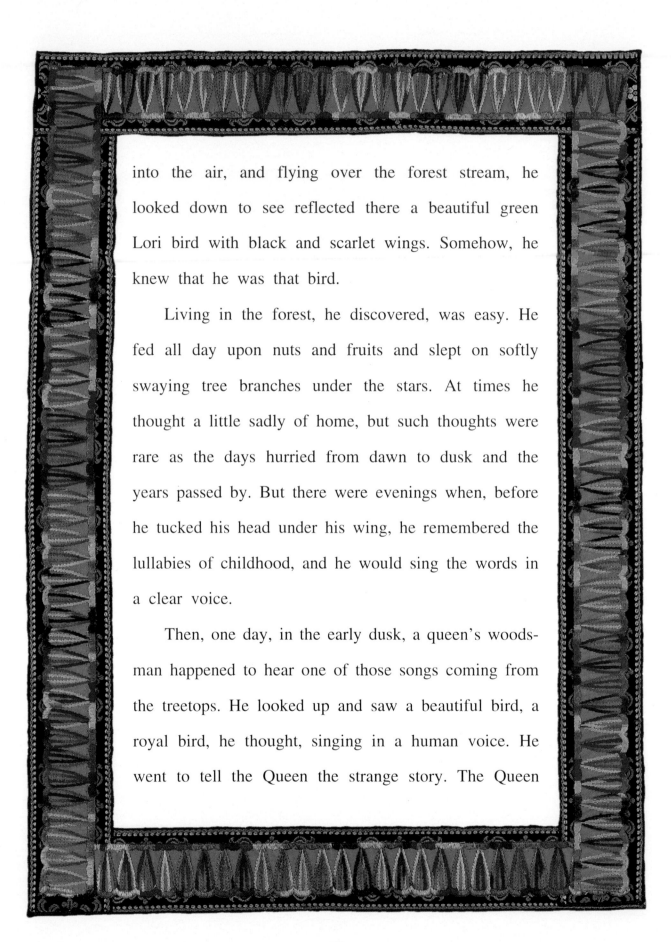

into the air, and flying over the forest stream, he looked down to see reflected there a beautiful green Lori bird with black and scarlet wings. Somehow, he knew that he was that bird.

Living in the forest, he discovered, was easy. He fed all day upon nuts and fruits and slept on softly swaying tree branches under the stars. At times he thought a little sadly of home, but such thoughts were rare as the days hurried from dawn to dusk and the years passed by. But there were evenings when, before he tucked his head under his wing, he remembered the lullabies of childhood, and he would sing the words in a clear voice.

Then, one day, in the early dusk, a queen's woodsman happened to hear one of those songs coming from the treetops. He looked up and saw a beautiful bird, a royal bird, he thought, singing in a human voice. He went to tell the Queen the strange story. The Queen

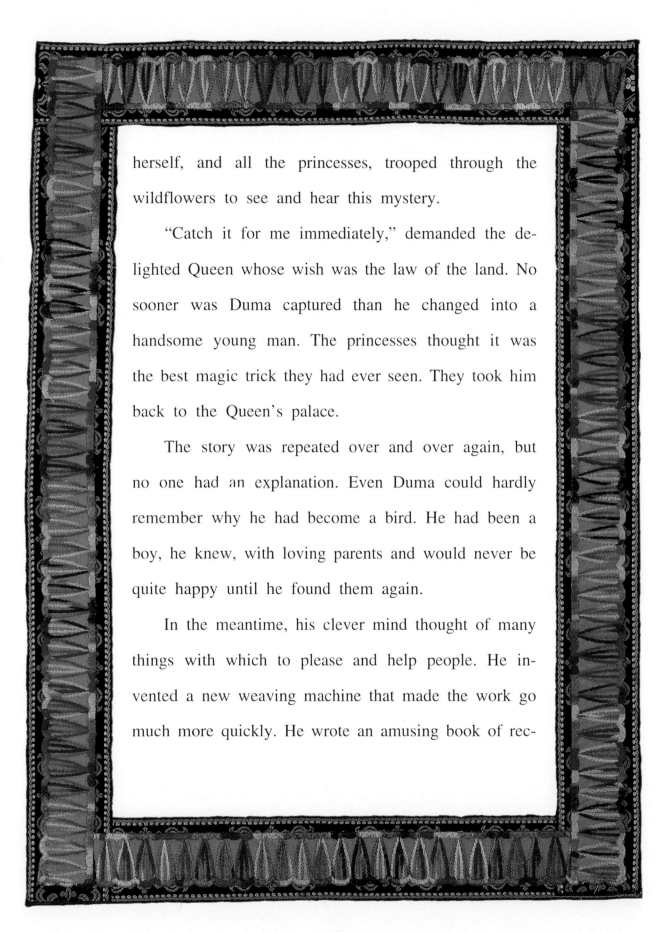

herself, and all the princesses, trooped through the wildflowers to see and hear this mystery.

"Catch it for me immediately," demanded the delighted Queen whose wish was the law of the land. No sooner was Duma captured than he changed into a handsome young man. The princesses thought it was the best magic trick they had ever seen. They took him back to the Queen's palace.

The story was repeated over and over again, but no one had an explanation. Even Duma could hardly remember why he had become a bird. He had been a boy, he knew, with loving parents and would never be quite happy until he found them again.

In the meantime, his clever mind thought of many things with which to please and help people. He invented a new weaving machine that made the work go much more quickly. He wrote an amusing book of recipes using goat's milk and created a flute that duplicated bird's songs perfectly.

Then it happened. A wise old man visited the Queen's court and recalled that many years ago a couple had visited him in search of their lost little son. They had told of a fantastic blue bird that granted wishes and of how their small field, because of such a wish, produced food in magical abundance. In fact, the pair did not live very far away and were the most skilled gardeners in the land.

It was only a short time before Duma and his parents were reunited. When he saw them he remembered all of his childhood in an instant. There were many tearful and loving embraces.

"What happened to you? How did you live?" his parents asked when they had somewhat recovered themselves.

"I became a bird," replied Duma.

His mother looked surprised.

"Once you were a spider," she said after careful thought, "and ate a fly."

"And once you were a small green snake," added his father.

"But now I am your son again," said Duma, smiling, "and we will always be a family."

HAWAIIAN MAGIC

Hawaii

One day, when Hawaii was young, a little girl called Hina splashed about in the shallow water off the coast of a small island. She was tending to her garden of sea pansies and ancmones and arranging pink shell borders around them.

She moved back to avoid stepping on a spiny sea urchin when a squeaky, unused voice cried, "Watch out!"

Looking down through the shimmering water, she saw a blue sea star that had lost an arm not long before. The severed arm lay nearby. Perhaps the sea star had been in an accident. To her astonishment, it grew

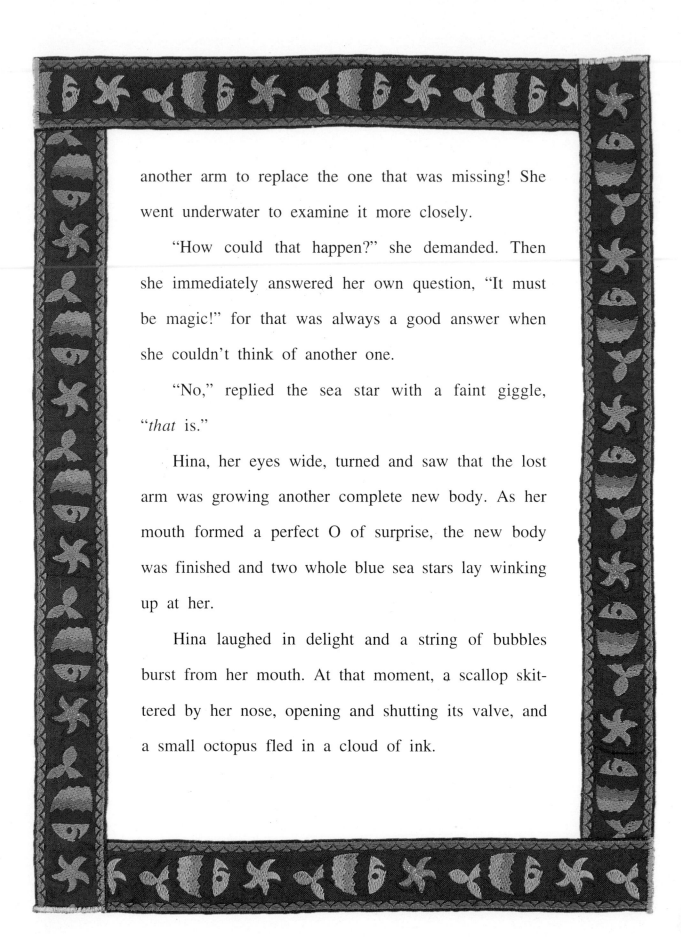

another arm to replace the one that was missing! She went underwater to examine it more closely.

"How could that happen?" she demanded. Then she immediately answered her own question, "It must be magic!" for that was always a good answer when she couldn't think of another one.

"No," replied the sea star with a faint giggle, "*that* is."

Hina, her eyes wide, turned and saw that the lost arm was growing another complete new body. As her mouth formed a perfect O of surprise, the new body was finished and two whole blue sea stars lay winking up at her.

Hina laughed in delight and a string of bubbles burst from her mouth. At that moment, a scallop skittered by her nose, opening and shutting its valve, and a small octopus fled in a cloud of ink.

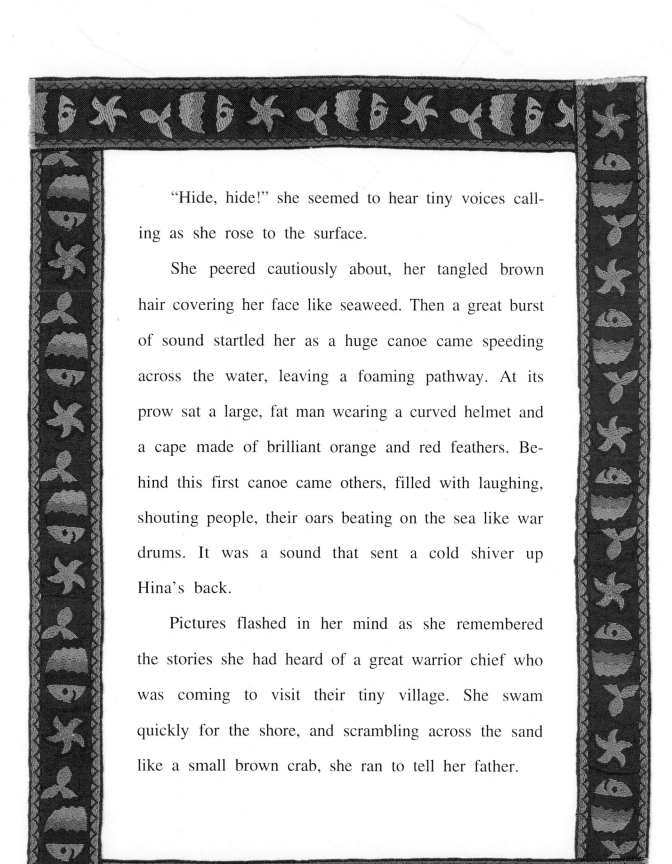

"Hide, hide!" she seemed to hear tiny voices calling as she rose to the surface.

She peered cautiously about, her tangled brown hair covering her face like seaweed. Then a great burst of sound startled her as a huge canoe came speeding across the water, leaving a foaming pathway. At its prow sat a large, fat man wearing a curved helmet and a cape made of brilliant orange and red feathers. Behind this first canoe came others, filled with laughing, shouting people, their oars beating on the sea like war drums. It was a sound that sent a cold shiver up Hina's back.

Pictures flashed in her mind as she remembered the stories she had heard of a great warrior chief who was coming to visit their tiny village. She swam quickly for the shore, and scrambling across the sand like a small brown crab, she ran to tell her father.

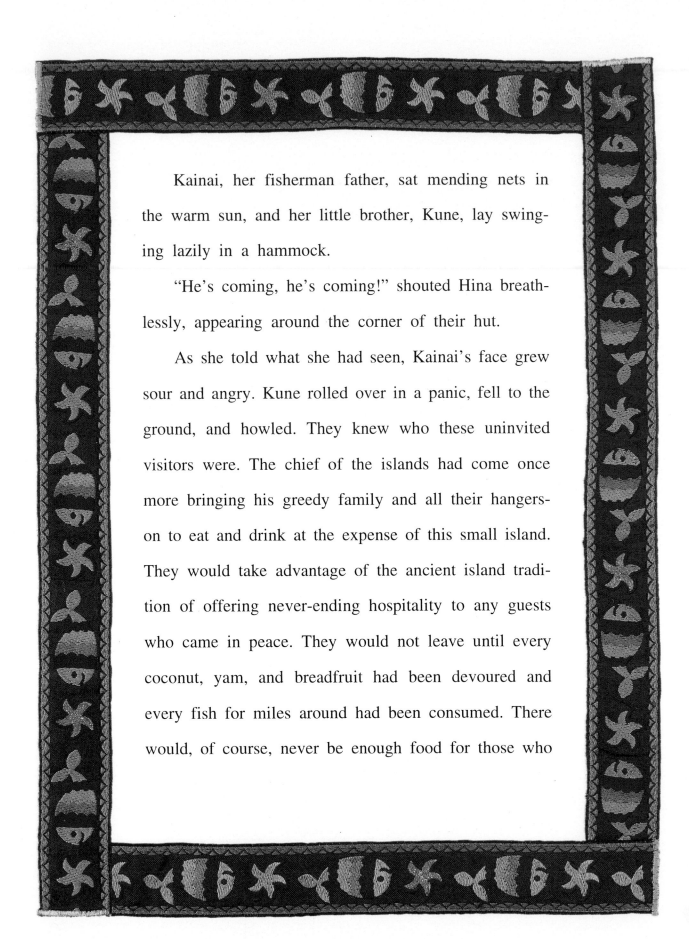

Kainai, her fisherman father, sat mending nets in the warm sun, and her little brother, Kune, lay swinging lazily in a hammock.

"He's coming, he's coming!" shouted Hina breathlessly, appearing around the corner of their hut.

As she told what she had seen, Kainai's face grew sour and angry. Kune rolled over in a panic, fell to the ground, and howled. They knew who these uninvited visitors were. The chief of the islands had come once more bringing his greedy family and all their hangers-on to eat and drink at the expense of this small island. They would take advantage of the ancient island tradition of offering never-ending hospitality to any guests who came in peace. They would not leave until every coconut, yam, and breadfruit had been devoured and every fish for miles around had been consumed. There would, of course, never be enough food for those who

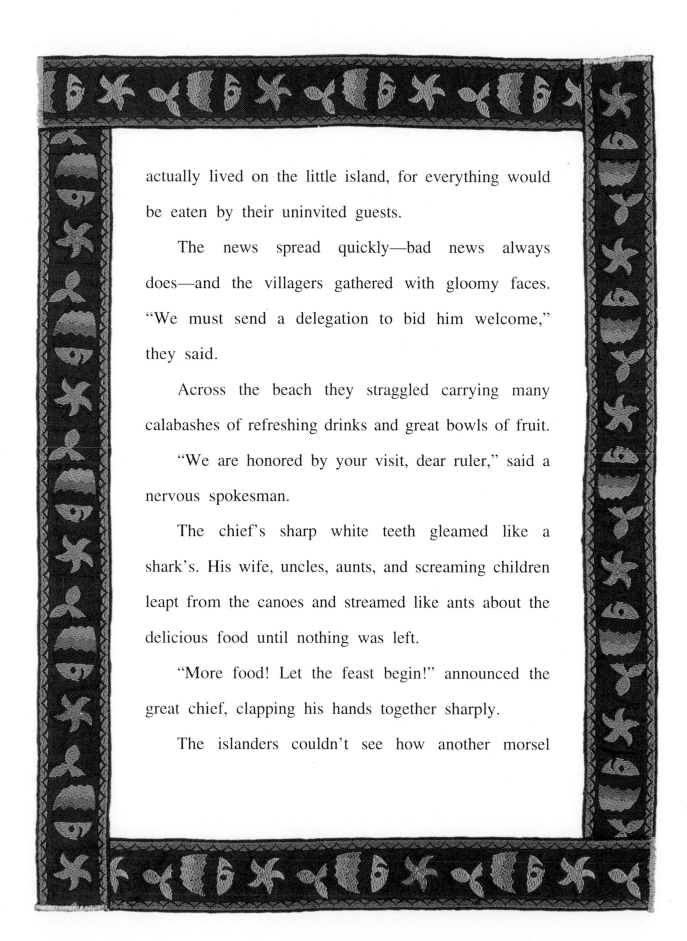

actually lived on the little island, for everything would be eaten by their uninvited guests.

The news spread quickly—bad news always does—and the villagers gathered with gloomy faces. "We must send a delegation to bid him welcome," they said.

Across the beach they straggled carrying many calabashes of refreshing drinks and great bowls of fruit.

"We are honored by your visit, dear ruler," said a nervous spokesman.

The chief's sharp white teeth gleamed like a shark's. His wife, uncles, aunts, and screaming children leapt from the canoes and streamed like ants about the delicious food until nothing was left.

"More food! Let the feast begin!" announced the great chief, clapping his hands together sharply.

The islanders couldn't see how another morsel

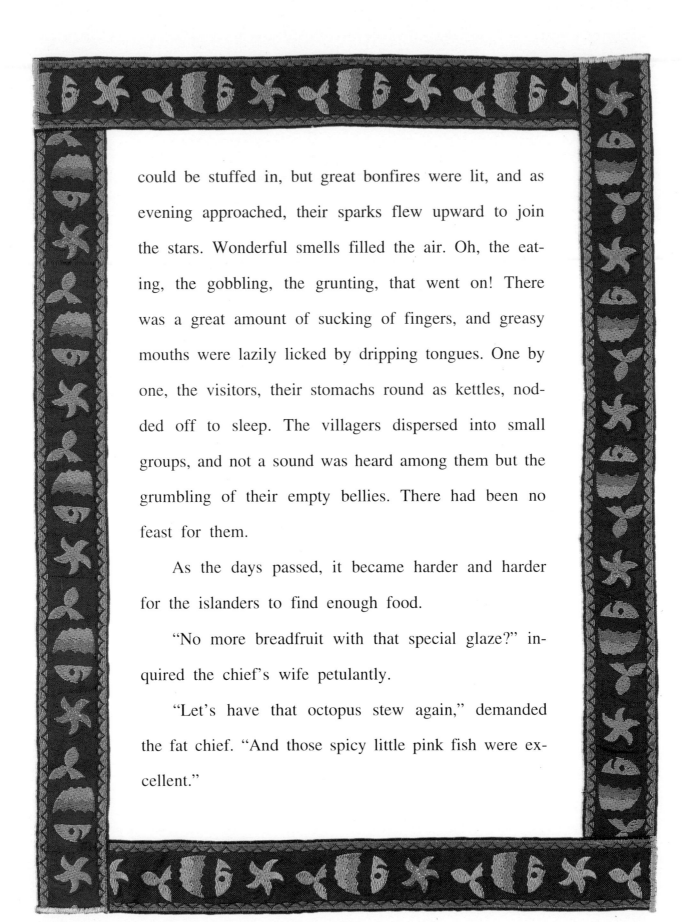

could be stuffed in, but great bonfires were lit, and as evening approached, their sparks flew upward to join the stars. Wonderful smells filled the air. Oh, the eating, the gobbling, the grunting, that went on! There was a great amount of sucking of fingers, and greasy mouths were lazily licked by dripping tongues. One by one, the visitors, their stomachs round as kettles, nodded off to sleep. The villagers dispersed into small groups, and not a sound was heard among them but the grumbling of their empty bellies. There had been no feast for them.

As the days passed, it became harder and harder for the islanders to find enough food.

"No more breadfruit with that special glaze?" inquired the chief's wife petulantly.

"Let's have that octopus stew again," demanded the fat chief. "And those spicy little pink fish were excellent."

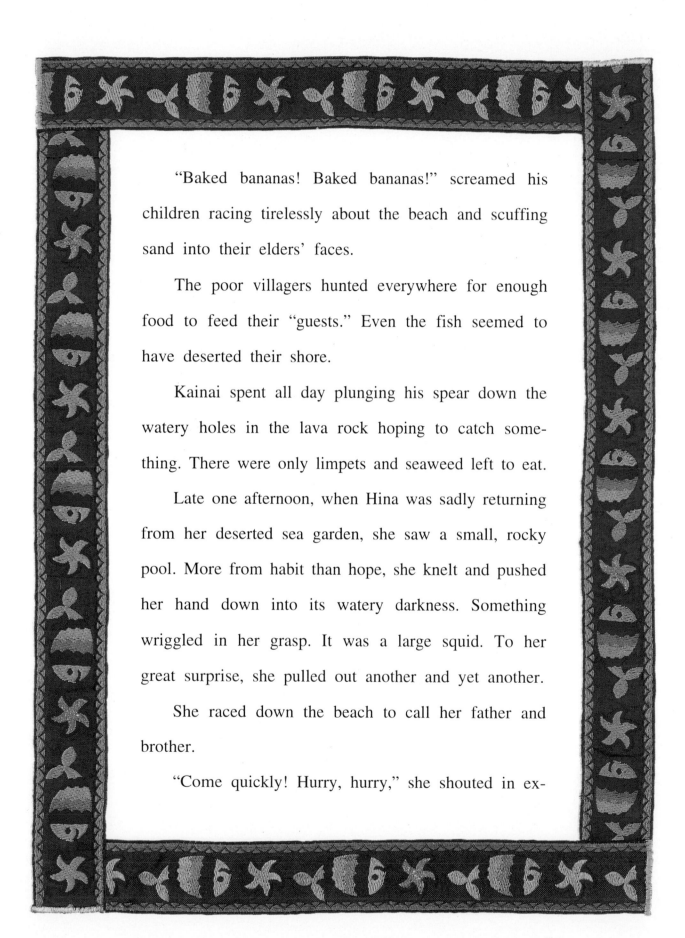

"Baked bananas! Baked bananas!" screamed his children racing tirelessly about the beach and scuffing sand into their elders' faces.

The poor villagers hunted everywhere for enough food to feed their "guests." Even the fish seemed to have deserted their shore.

Kainai spent all day plunging his spear down the watery holes in the lava rock hoping to catch something. There were only limpets and seaweed left to eat.

Late one afternoon, when Hina was sadly returning from her deserted sea garden, she saw a small, rocky pool. More from habit than hope, she knelt and pushed her hand down into its watery darkness. Something wriggled in her grasp. It was a large squid. To her great surprise, she pulled out another and yet another.

She raced down the beach to call her father and brother.

"Come quickly! Hurry, hurry," she shouted in ex-

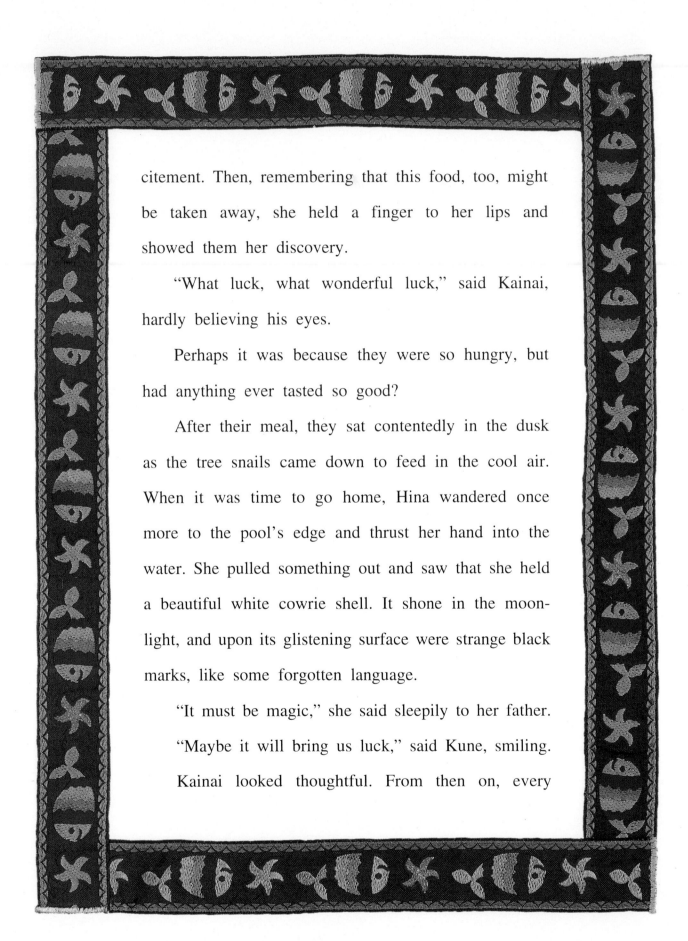

citement. Then, remembering that this food, too, might be taken away, she held a finger to her lips and showed them her discovery.

"What luck, what wonderful luck," said Kainai, hardly believing his eyes.

Perhaps it was because they were so hungry, but had anything ever tasted so good?

After their meal, they sat contentedly in the dusk as the tree snails came down to feed in the cool air. When it was time to go home, Hina wandered once more to the pool's edge and thrust her hand into the water. She pulled something out and saw that she held a beautiful white cowrie shell. It shone in the moonlight, and upon its glistening surface were strange black marks, like some forgotten language.

"It must be magic," she said sleepily to her father.

"Maybe it will bring us luck," said Kune, smiling.

Kainai looked thoughtful. From then on, every

morning he tied the shell to his fishing line and never returned empty-handed. The villagers shared his catch and perhaps his luck too, but no one mentioned the cowrie shell. Every night it lay hidden in a giant clamshell. Sometimes the children would take it out and stare at the marks on it. It almost seemed as if it could be read and its secret discovered, but they were always disappointed.

The warrior chief was pleasantly surprised. Although the fruits and vegetables had long since disappeared, there seemed to be an unending supply of the rarest and most delicious fish for his banquet. It was not long before he also discovered that Kainai was the fisherman who provided most of them. When one of the villagers was questioned and told that his nose might be cut off for crab bait, he admitted that Hina, Kainai's daughter, had been heard to use the world "magic" quite often.

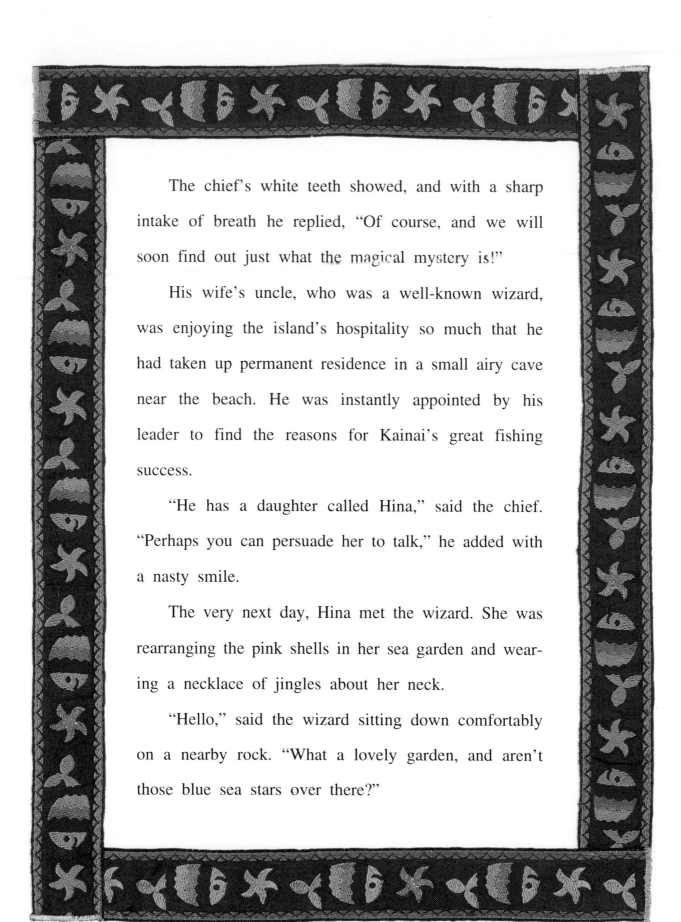

The chief's white teeth showed, and with a sharp intake of breath he replied, "Of course, and we will soon find out just what the magical mystery is!"

His wife's uncle, who was a well-known wizard, was enjoying the island's hospitality so much that he had taken up permanent residence in a small airy cave near the beach. He was instantly appointed by his leader to find the reasons for Kainai's great fishing success.

"He has a daughter called Hina," said the chief. "Perhaps you can persuade her to talk," he added with a nasty smile.

The very next day, Hina met the wizard. She was rearranging the pink shells in her sea garden and wearing a necklace of jingles about her neck.

"Hello," said the wizard sitting down comfortably on a nearby rock. "What a lovely garden, and aren't those blue sea stars over there?"

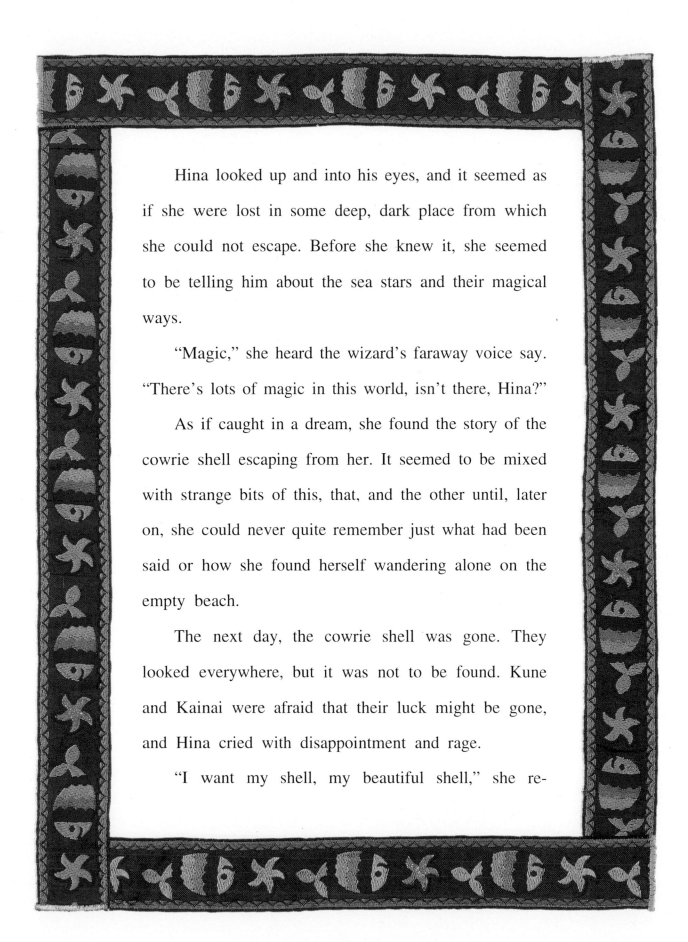

Hina looked up and into his eyes, and it seemed as if she were lost in some deep, dark place from which she could not escape. Before she knew it, she seemed to be telling him about the sea stars and their magical ways.

"Magic," she heard the wizard's faraway voice say. "There's lots of magic in this world, isn't there, Hina?"

As if caught in a dream, she found the story of the cowrie shell escaping from her. It seemed to be mixed with strange bits of this, that, and the other until, later on, she could never quite remember just what had been said or how she found herself wandering alone on the empty beach.

The next day, the cowrie shell was gone. They looked everywhere, but it was not to be found. Kune and Kainai were afraid that their luck might be gone, and Hina cried with disappointment and rage.

"I want my shell, my beautiful shell," she repeated, the tears making salty trails down her cheeks. But although she knew perfectly well who had taken it, somehow the words describing the stranger on the beach could not pass her lips. She looked for comfort in the warm ocean currents and each day found it harder and harder to leave the sea. The rainbow-colored jellyfish drifted past her and the dolphins bumped her with their round heads. It was not until one evening, while she floated looking upward, that a small blue star in the sky reminded her of her other friends, the blue sea stars. She returned to her garden early the next morning and dived down through the turquoise water to talk to her old friends.

There must have been a great deal said, for bubbles, large and small, rose steadily. Some of them burst, and little squeaks and laughs were heard. When Hina finally surfaced, her face was filled with a kind

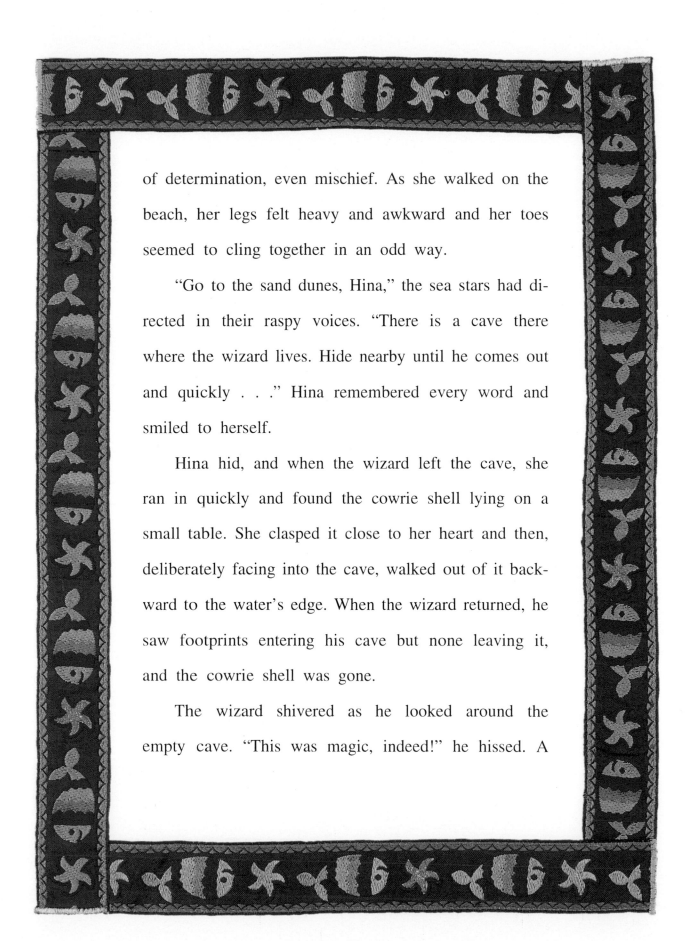

of determination, even mischief. As she walked on the beach, her legs felt heavy and awkward and her toes seemed to cling together in an odd way.

"Go to the sand dunes, Hina," the sea stars had directed in their raspy voices. "There is a cave there where the wizard lives. Hide nearby until he comes out and quickly . . ." Hina remembered every word and smiled to herself.

Hina hid, and when the wizard left the cave, she ran in quickly and found the cowrie shell lying on a small table. She clasped it close to her heart and then, deliberately facing into the cave, walked out of it backward to the water's edge. When the wizard returned, he saw footprints entering his cave but none leaving it, and the cowrie shell was gone.

The wizard shivered as he looked around the empty cave. "This was magic, indeed!" he hissed. A

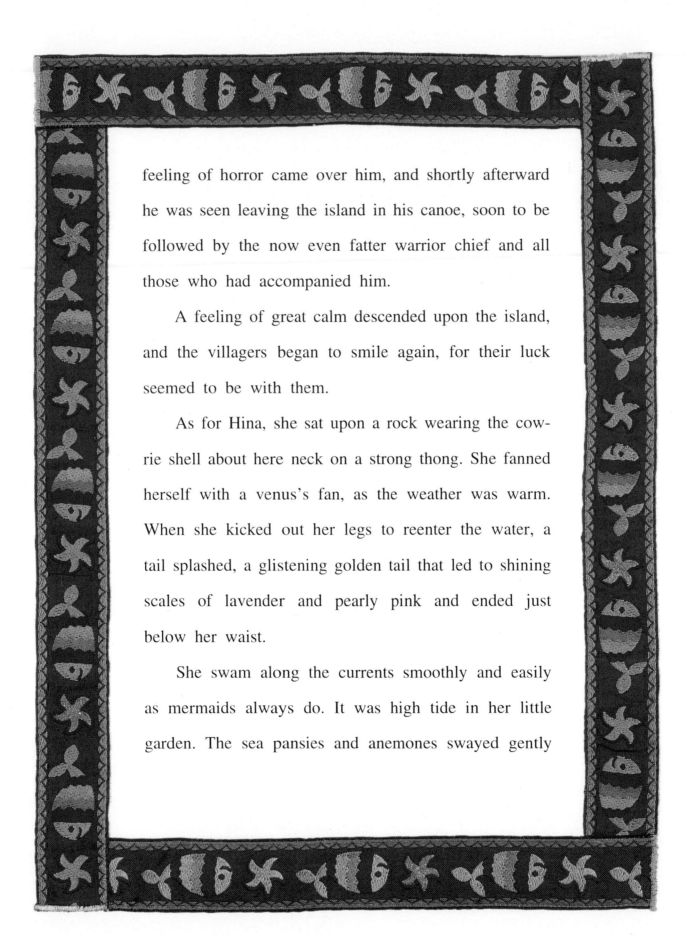

feeling of horror came over him, and shortly afterward he was seen leaving the island in his canoe, soon to be followed by the now even fatter warrior chief and all those who had accompanied him.

A feeling of great calm descended upon the island, and the villagers began to smile again, for their luck seemed to be with them.

As for Hina, she sat upon a rock wearing the cowrie shell about here neck on a strong thong. She fanned herself with a venus's fan, as the weather was warm. When she kicked out her legs to reenter the water, a tail splashed, a glistening golden tail that led to shining scales of lavender and pearly pink and ended just below her waist.

She swam along the currents smoothly and easily as mermaids always do. It was high tide in her little garden. The sea pansies and anemones swayed gently

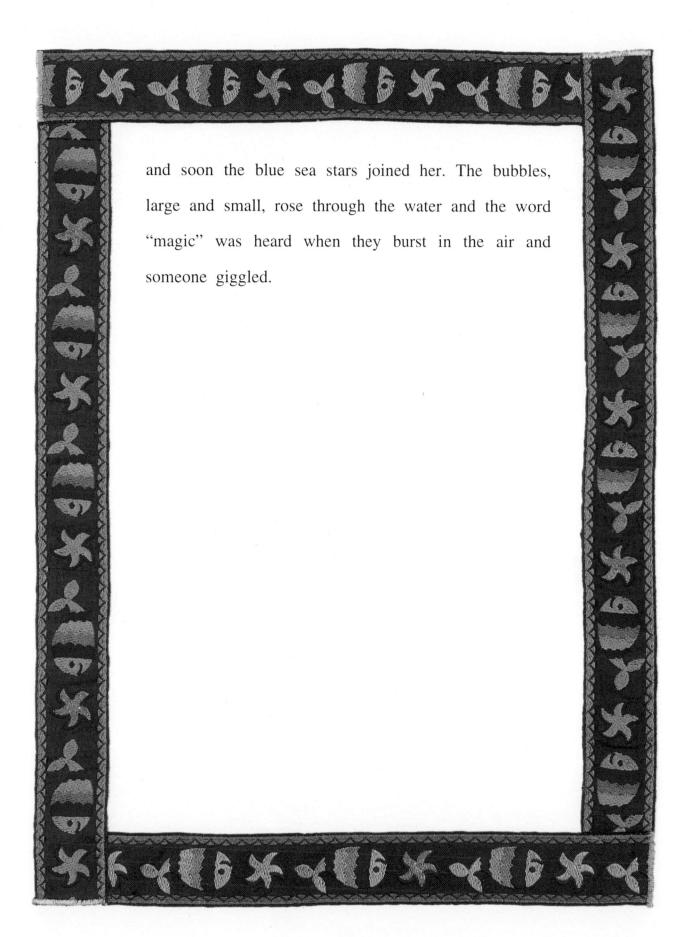

and soon the blue sea stars joined her. The bubbles, large and small, rose through the water and the word "magic" was heard when they burst in the air and someone giggled.

RED DRAGON BLUE DRAGON

China

*I*n the deep ocean, lived two sea dragons. Mr. Dragon was a beautiful, shin-
ing blue. His claws were gold and his eyes were like
flashing rubies. Mrs. Dragon was the flickering red of
a glowing fire, her eyes of sapphire, and each of her
claws was tipped with diamond. They lived a carefree
life feeding on opals and pearls and except for small
chores, like guarding hidden treasures, thought of nothing but their own pleasure and enjoyment. They pur-
sued this happy existence until one fateful day when
Mr. Dragon noticed that his wife's brilliant red scales
had faded to a dull pink; her blue eyes had dimmed
and her gaze was unfocused.

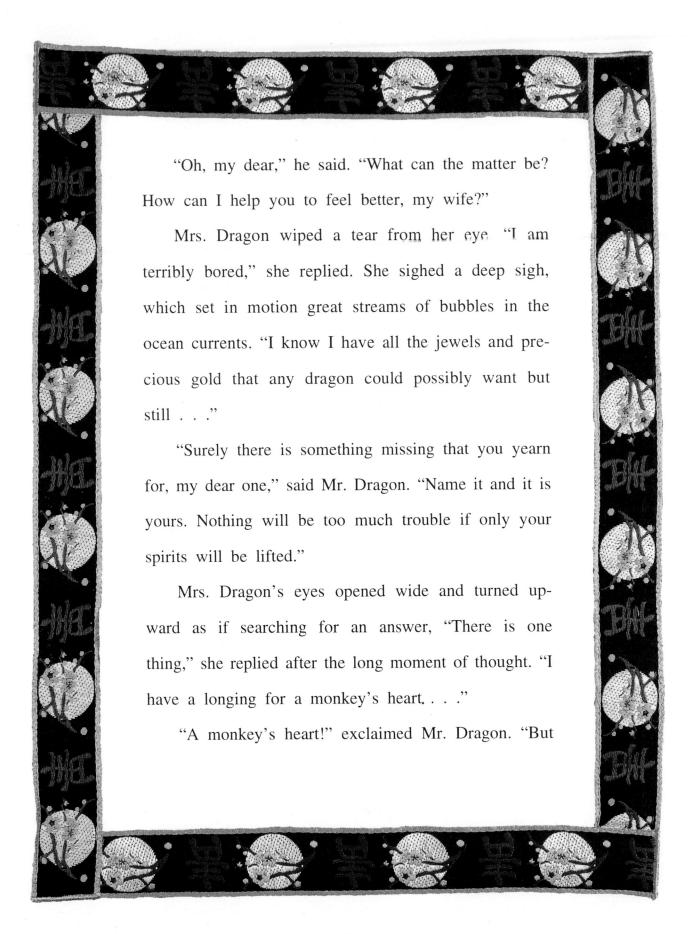

"Oh, my dear," he said. "What can the matter be? How can I help you to feel better, my wife?"

Mrs. Dragon wiped a tear from her eye. "I am terribly bored," she replied. She sighed a deep sigh, which set in motion great streams of bubbles in the ocean currents. "I know I have all the jewels and precious gold that any dragon could possibly want but still . . ."

"Surely there is something missing that you yearn for, my dear one," said Mr. Dragon. "Name it and it is yours. Nothing will be too much trouble if only your spirits will be lifted."

Mrs. Dragon's eyes opened wide and turned upward as if searching for an answer, "There is one thing," she replied after the long moment of thought. "I have a longing for a monkey's heart. . . ."

"A monkey's heart!" exclaimed Mr. Dragon. "But

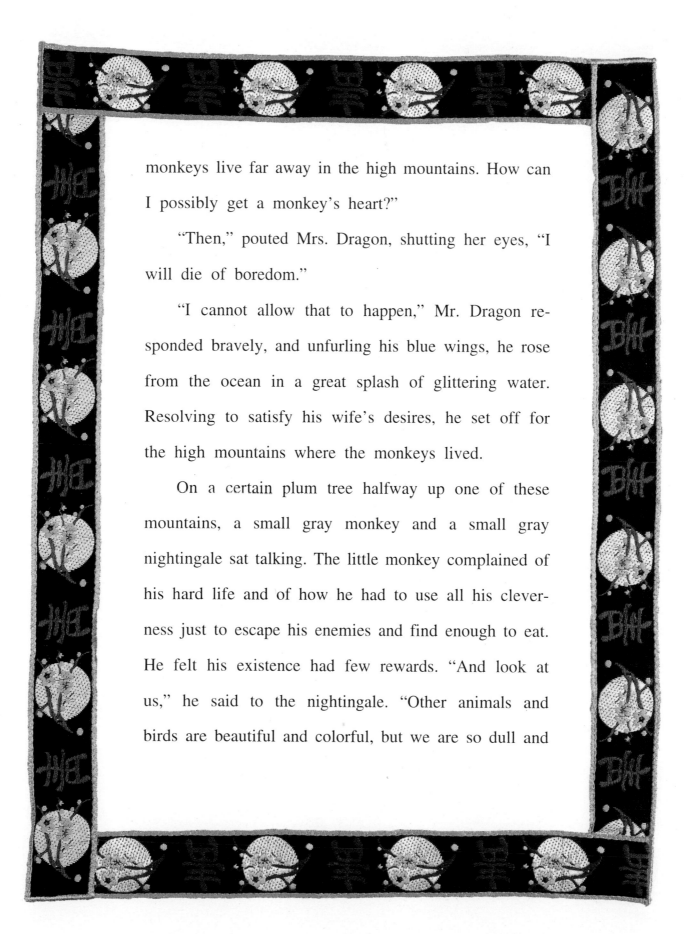

monkeys live far away in the high mountains. How can I possibly get a monkey's heart?"

"Then," pouted Mrs. Dragon, shutting her eyes, "I will die of boredom."

"I cannot allow that to happen," Mr. Dragon responded bravely, and unfurling his blue wings, he rose from the ocean in a great splash of glittering water. Resolving to satisfy his wife's desires, he set off for the high mountains where the monkeys lived.

On a certain plum tree halfway up one of these mountains, a small gray monkey and a small gray nightingale sat talking. The little monkey complained of his hard life and of how he had to use all his cleverness just to escape his enemies and find enough to eat. He felt his existence had few rewards. "And look at us," he said to the nightingale. "Other animals and birds are beautiful and colorful, but we are so dull and

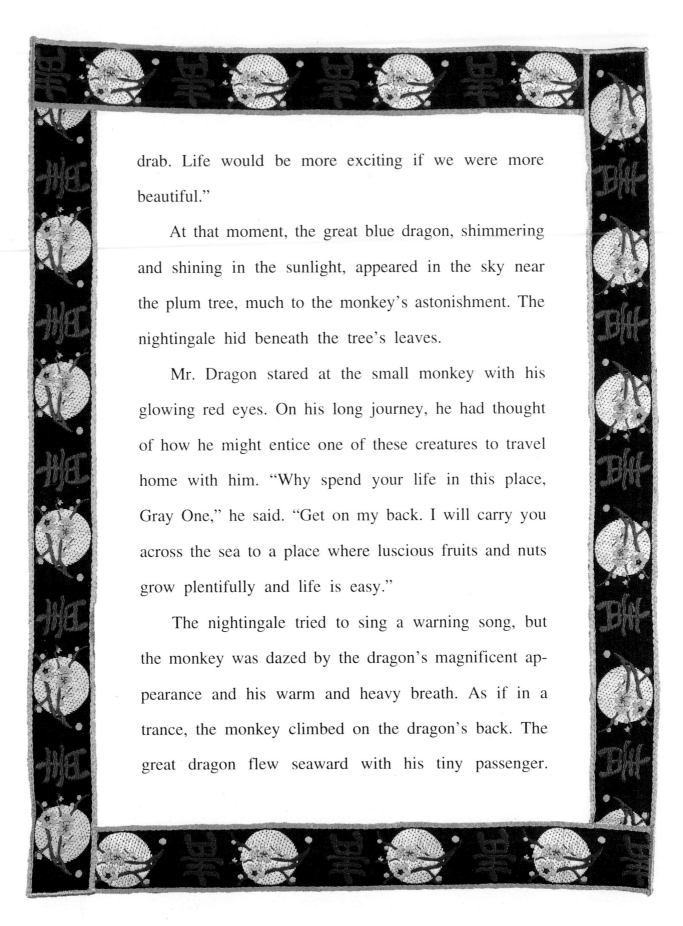

drab. Life would be more exciting if we were more beautiful."

At that moment, the great blue dragon, shimmering and shining in the sunlight, appeared in the sky near the plum tree, much to the monkey's astonishment. The nightingale hid beneath the tree's leaves.

Mr. Dragon stared at the small monkey with his glowing red eyes. On his long journey, he had thought of how he might entice one of these creatures to travel home with him. "Why spend your life in this place, Gray One," he said. "Get on my back. I will carry you across the sea to a place where luscious fruits and nuts grow plentifully and life is easy."

The nightingale tried to sing a warning song, but the monkey was dazed by the dragon's magnificent ap-pearance and his warm and heavy breath. As if in a trance, the monkey climbed on the dragon's back. The great dragon flew seaward with his tiny passenger.

Suddenly, he dipped over the ocean until the sea foam flew into the monkey's face.

"Where are we going?" the monkey screamed in alarm.

"Oh, dear friend, my wife is fading away from boredom and nothing will revive her but a monkey's heart."

"What shall I do?" thought the monkey. "Great Blue One," he cried over the roar of the ocean's waves, "you should have told me before. I left my heart hanging at the top of my tree. Take me back and I will fetch it for you."

The dragon flew back to the top of the plum tree and dropped off his passenger. As he was too large to sit in trees, he landed on the ground beneath it and waited impatiently. The nightingale was at the top of the tree hoping that his clever monkey friend might somehow return. She listened as the monkey quickly explained his predicament and then whispered in his ear. Nightingales are wise as well as musical.

"Hurry up!" shouted the dragon. "Mrs. Dragon is waiting."

"Here you are, old wise one," said the monkey as he dropped one of the plums from his tree to the ground.

Off flew the dragon clutching this precious "monkey's heart" only to find Mrs. Dragon much improved when he arrived. Mrs. Dragon, being rather fickle, had already thought of a new cure for her listlessness. She ate the "monkey's heart" without much interest.

"What I really want," she informed her tired husband, her eyes glowing with excitement, "is a necklace of tiger's claws."

"Of course, my dear," answered Mr. Dragon, feeling very out of sorts. It had been an exhausting day.

From that day on, the monkey was quite satisfied to be clever and gray and to make his own life as exciting as he wished it to be. As for the colorful dragons, they bored themselves to extinction.

This story was adapted from part of the Gautama Buddha legend.

THE TURQUOISE SANDALS

Egypt

Once, long ago in Egypt, an old Greek merchant called Charaxes was walking in the market square not far from where he lived. There were all sorts of things for sale—dates, figs, almonds, funny monkeys, cats, and exquisite birds in gilded cages—and among all the color and confusion a slave auction was being held. Charaxes pushed through the crowd and saw that a beautiful young girl with golden hair and pink tear-stained cheeks was being sold. The story was told that she had been captured by pirates while still a child and now was on the auction block because her master needed money.

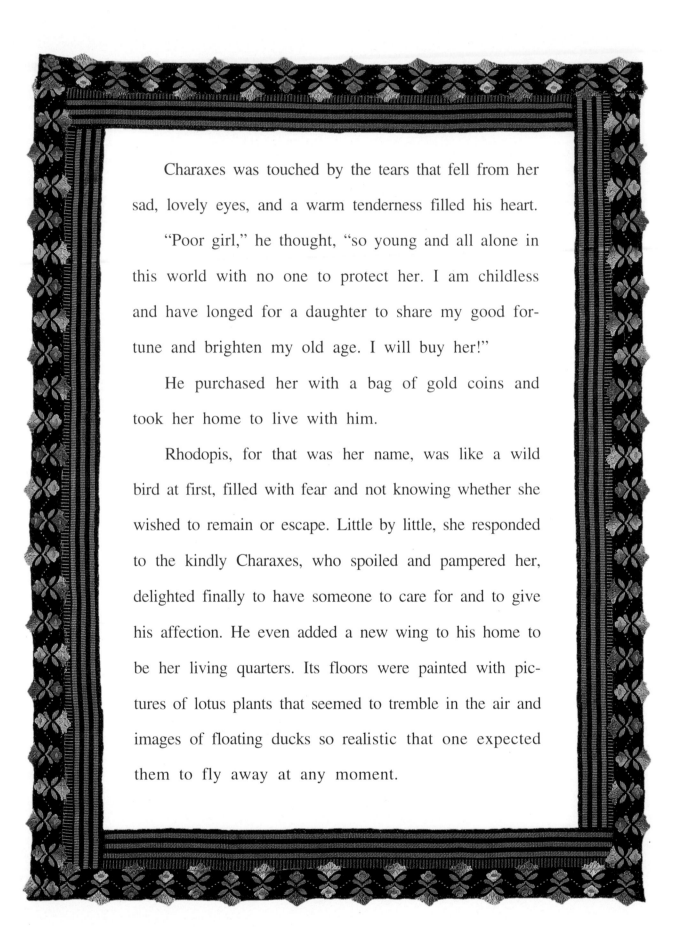

Charaxes was touched by the tears that fell from her sad, lovely eyes, and a warm tenderness filled his heart.

"Poor girl," he thought, "so young and all alone in this world with no one to protect her. I am childless and have longed for a daughter to share my good fortune and brighten my old age. I will buy her!"

He purchased her with a bag of gold coins and took her home to live with him.

Rhodopis, for that was her name, was like a wild bird at first, filled with fear and not knowing whether she wished to remain or escape. Little by little, she responded to the kindly Charaxes, who spoiled and pampered her, delighted finally to have someone to care for and to give his affection. He even added a new wing to his home to be her living quarters. Its floors were painted with pictures of lotus plants that seemed to tremble in the air and images of floating ducks so realistic that one expected them to fly away at any moment.

Just outside her bedroom door was a garden filled with elegant trees. Beds of rare flowers filled the air with delightful smells. A large pool, with water that exactly matched the blue of the sky, lay waiting for her to enter it. When the warmth of the day tired her, Rhodopis would go bathing there. Then other, less fortunate slave girls would massage her with rare oils until she fell asleep.

"Here, my dear," Charaxes would call as he bustled back from the marketplace, "some delicious sweetmeats," and he would pop one into her mouth as if she were one of the caged birds that hung everywhere in the house and who were allowed no existence other than that of being beautiful.

"Oh, thank you, dear Charaxes," Rhodopis would murmur in her soft, dovelike voice. "You are too good." She could never be unkind to Charaxes, who only wished to make her happy.

Sometimes she would say hesitantly, "Have you found any more papyrus rolls for me to read? I do so love the stories of far-off places and the maps, and even the monsters."

In her young life, sad as it had been, she had learned both to read and to write. Learning about the world she could never see remained her chief delight. The scrolls she read were like magical doors that could open up all sorts of experiences of mind and heart that a slave girl could never expect to actually experience herself.

Poor Charaxes knew a great deal about making money and the world of business but very little about a girl like Rhodopis. Her first master had been a learned man who had taught her to read and write. Charaxes thought of her as a charming pet to be spoiled and pampered, not as the intelligent and coura-geous girl that she was.

"Read?" he would say in astonishment. "Don't

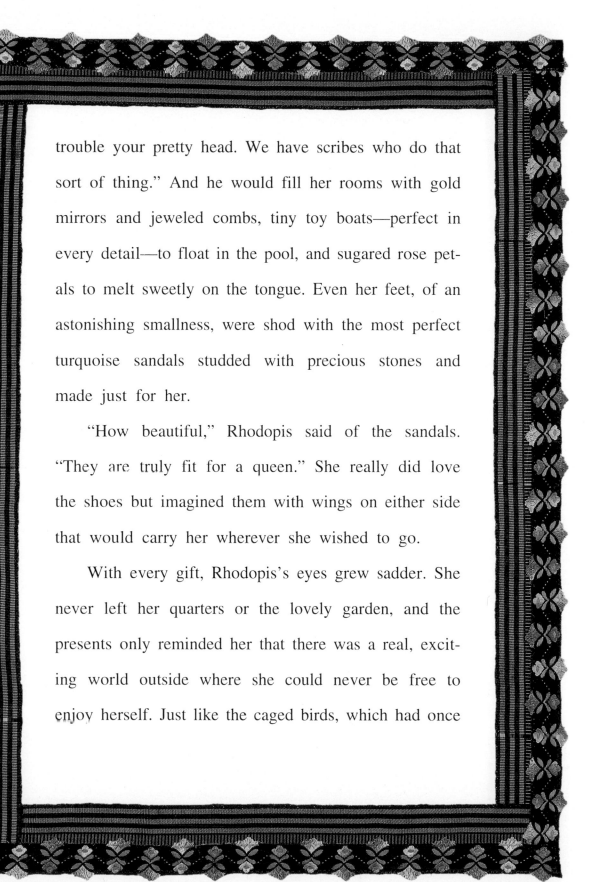

trouble your pretty head. We have scribes who do that sort of thing." And he would fill her rooms with gold mirrors and jeweled combs, tiny toy boats—perfect in every detail—to float in the pool, and sugared rose petals to melt sweetly on the tongue. Even her feet, of an astonishing smallness, were shod with the most perfect turquoise sandals studded with precious stones and made just for her.

"How beautiful," Rhodopis said of the sandals. "They are truly fit for a queen." She really did love the shoes but imagined them with wings on either side that would carry her wherever she wished to go.

With every gift, Rhodopis's eyes grew sadder. She never left her quarters or the lovely garden, and the presents only reminded her that there was a real, exciting world outside where she could never be free to enjoy herself. Just like the caged birds, which had once

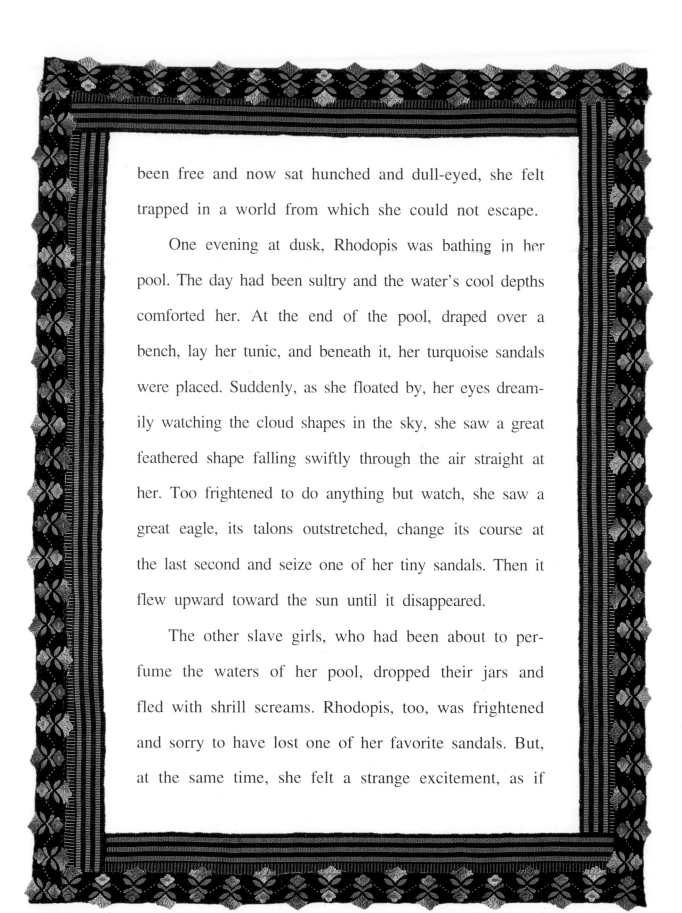

been free and now sat hunched and dull-eyed, she felt trapped in a world from which she could not escape.

One evening at dusk, Rhodopis was bathing in her pool. The day had been sultry and the water's cool depths comforted her. At the end of the pool, draped over a bench, lay her tunic, and beneath it, her turquoise sandals were placed. Suddenly, as she floated by, her eyes dreamily watching the cloud shapes in the sky, she saw a great feathered shape falling swiftly through the air straight at her. Too frightened to do anything but watch, she saw a great eagle, its talons outstretched, change its course at the last second and seize one of her tiny sandals. Then it flew upward toward the sun until it disappeared.

The other slave girls, who had been about to perfume the waters of her pool, dropped their jars and fled with shrill screams. Rhodopis, too, was frightened and sorry to have lost one of her favorite sandals. But, at the same time, she felt a strange excitement, as if

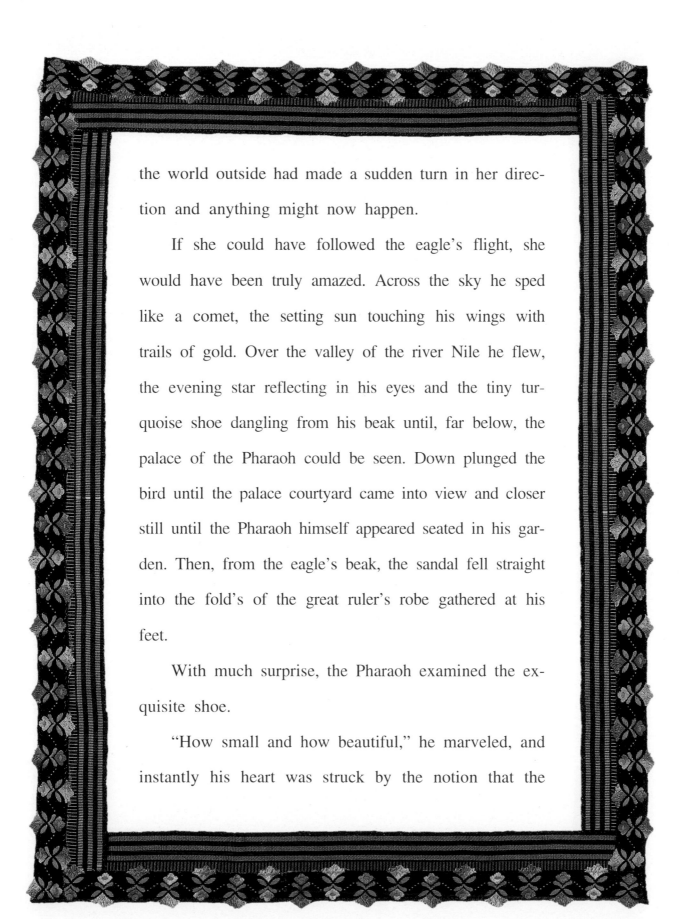

the world outside had made a sudden turn in her direction and anything might now happen.

If she could have followed the eagle's flight, she would have been truly amazed. Across the sky he sped like a comet, the setting sun touching his wings with trails of gold. Over the valley of the river Nile he flew, the evening star reflecting in his eyes and the tiny turquoise shoe dangling from his beak until, far below, the palace of the Pharaoh could be seen. Down plunged the bird until the palace courtyard came into view and closer still until the Pharaoh himself appeared seated in his garden. Then, from the eagle's beak, the sandal fell straight into the fold's of the great ruler's robe gathered at his feet.

With much surprise, the Pharaoh examined the exquisite shoe.

"How small and how beautiful," he marveled, and instantly his heart was struck by the notion that the

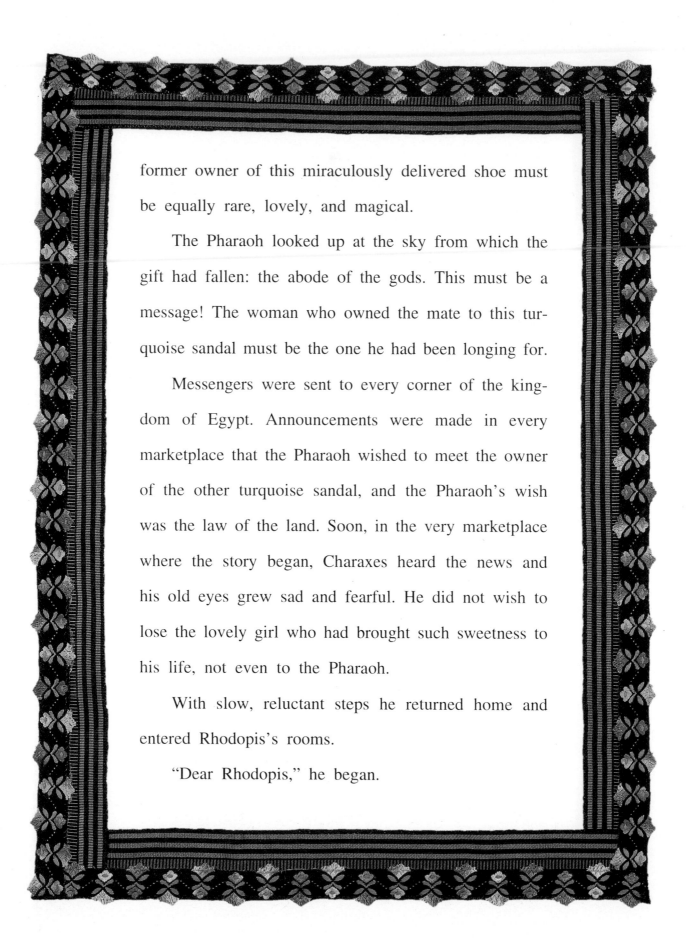

former owner of this miraculously delivered shoe must be equally rare, lovely, and magical.

The Pharaoh looked up at the sky from which the gift had fallen: the abode of the gods. This must be a message! The woman who owned the mate to this turquoise sandal must be the one he had been longing for.

Messengers were sent to every corner of the kingdom of Egypt. Announcements were made in every marketplace that the Pharaoh wished to meet the owner of the other turquoise sandal, and the Pharaoh's wish was the law of the land. Soon, in the very marketplace where the story began, Charaxes heard the news and his old eyes grew sad and fearful. He did not wish to lose the lovely girl who had brought such sweetness to his life, not even to the Pharaoh.

With slow, reluctant steps he returned home and entered Rhodopis's rooms.

"Dear Rhodopis," he began.

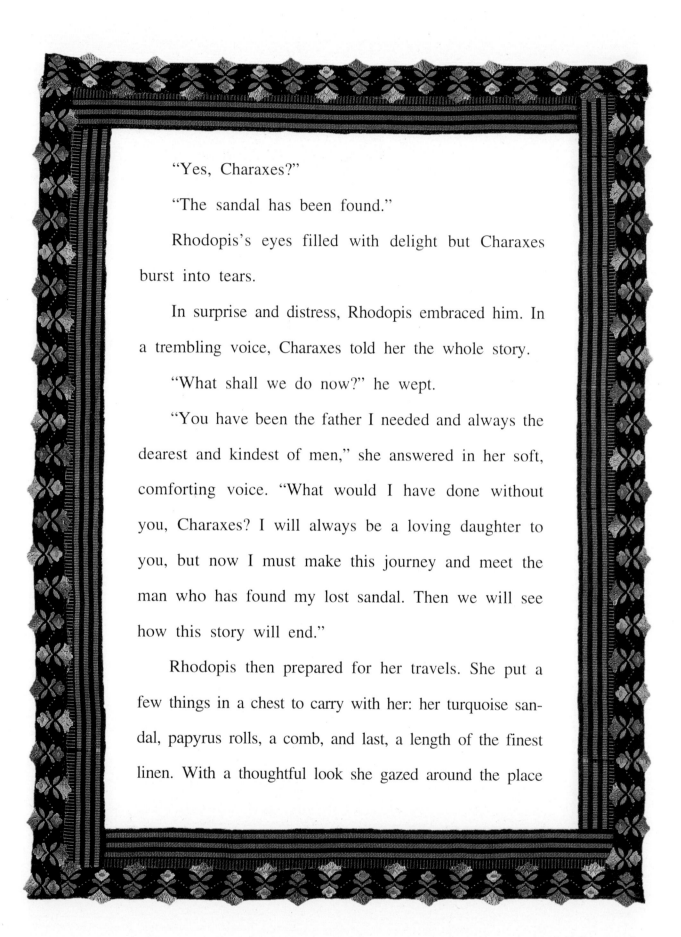

"Yes, Charaxes?"

"The sandal has been found."

Rhodopis's eyes filled with delight but Charaxes burst into tears.

In surprise and distress, Rhodopis embraced him. In a trembling voice, Charaxes told her the whole story.

"What shall we do now?" he wept.

"You have been the father I needed and always the dearest and kindest of men," she answered in her soft, comforting voice. "What would I have done without you, Charaxes? I will always be a loving daughter to you, but now I must make this journey and meet the man who has found my lost sandal. Then we will see how this story will end."

Rhodopis then prepared for her travels. She put a few things in a chest to carry with her: her turquoise sandal, papyrus rolls, a comb, and last, a length of the finest linen. With a thoughtful look she gazed around the place that had been her home. She was about to leave when, suddenly, she remembered something. She went to each bird's cage and opened the door to set it free.

She kissed her slave girls and Charaxes good-bye and left knowing the great world that had been shown to her in books must now open up to her. She wished to use this moment to its best advantage and never be a lovely caged bird again.

When at last Rhodopis met the Pharaoh, she was covered from head to foot in the length of gauzy linen through which nothing could be seen, only the small turquoise sandals on her feet. After carefully comparing the two matching sandals, one of the vizier's officials had returned the missing one to Rhodopis. She was determined not to let her beauty lead her into bondage once again. The Pharaoh, who was both surprised and amused, spent many weeks talking to this mysterious woman. Her shrouded mystery captured his interest.

As they exchanged ideas, the Pharaoh realized that Rhodopis was truly the woman of his dreams, and she, too, saw that he was not just a powerful ruler but a generous and intelligent man with whom she wished to spend the rest of her days. They both fell deeply in love.

On their wedding day, they stood before the assembled lords and ladies of the kingdom. The happy Charaxes suddenly realized that such a pair would have children he could spoil and love. Rhodopis finally revealed her face, but before he kissed her, the Pharaoh proclaimed that her beauty was only the outer reflection of her even more beautiful inner qualities. He and his new queen ruled over Egypt together for many happy years.

We cannot forget Rhodopis and her turquoise sandals, for she became the model for a fairy tale that took place many centuries later—a tale of a young girl who wore glass slippers and whose name was Cinderella.

THE CHAMELEON

Zaire

*L*ong, long ago, the story goes, there were a people called the Efe who came down from a place called the Mountains of the Moon in Africa to start new lives in the Ituri Forest. They were Pygmies, smaller than other tribespeople, but strong and brave and ready to start a new life. They were lead by a man called Grimli, who bore on his shoulders his infant son, Bingo, and wore about his waist a leather pouch holding magic stones that had fallen from the moon. These small black pebbles were powerful and were to be used only three times before being passed on to the next leader.

Times were hard for the Efe in the beginning. Although the forest was lush and green, everything was unknown. At first they were not sure which foods were edible or how to find fire when lightning struck. They did not even know how to build shelters, for they had lived in caves before. All the men, women, and children worked long days and slept short nights around the campfire. Grimli hurried everywhere counting and naming the animals. Irma, his wife and Bingo's mother, searched for and tested plants that might cure diseases. They all learned more and more, but they had not learned to smile, for life was too difficult. Still Grimli had not thought to use his magic stones.

Bingo grew older. His legs grew longer and his curiosity grew bigger by the day. He watched the grown-ups become so tired from hunting and gathering and working that they could think of nothing else. The other children were exact copies of their elders. They had not yet learned how to play. But Bingo, his brown

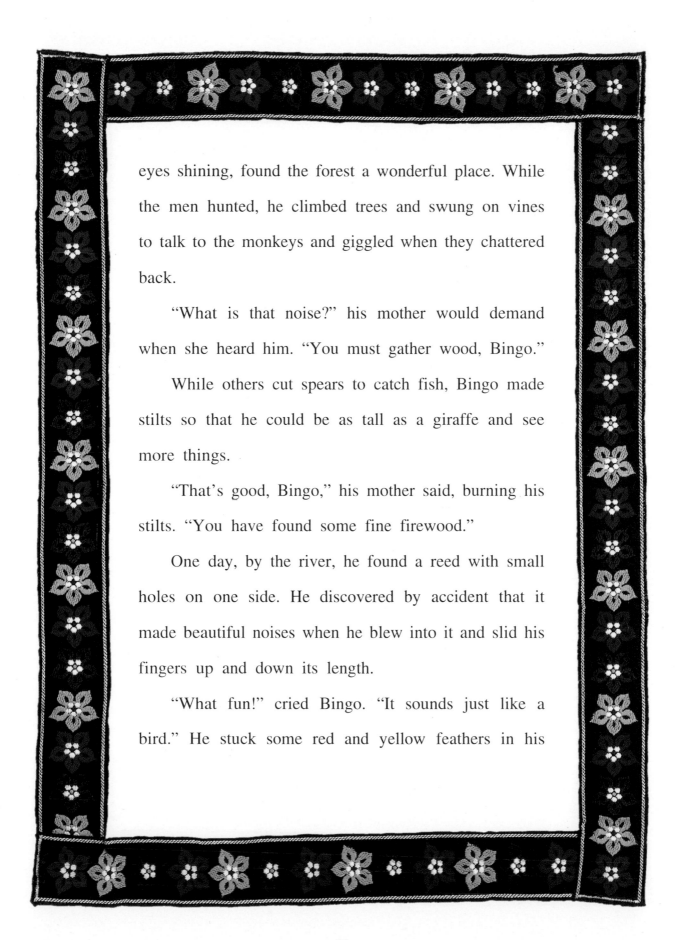

eyes shining, found the forest a wonderful place. While the men hunted, he climbed trees and swung on vines to talk to the monkeys and giggled when they chattered back.

"What is that noise?" his mother would demand when she heard him. "You must gather wood, Bingo."

While others cut spears to catch fish, Bingo made stilts so that he could be as tall as a giraffe and see more things.

"That's good, Bingo," his mother said, burning his stilts. "You have found some fine firewood."

One day, by the river, he found a reed with small holes on one side. He discovered by accident that it made beautiful noises when he blew into it and slid his fingers up and down its length.

"What fun!" cried Bingo. "It sounds just like a bird." He stuck some red and yellow feathers in his hair and sat on a low branch twittering his reed and pretending to be a bird.

A large red and green parrot with glowing yellow eyes dropped down to join him and started to talk. Bingo was not surprised, for the world was young and anything was possible.

"What sort of bird are you?" asked the parrot. "And what sort of a beak is that?" he added, staring at Bingo's nose.

"I am a boy-bird," answered Bingo, who had just invented a game called Let's Pretend and played a sweet little song on his reed.

"Where are your wings?" inquired the parrot.

Bingo flapped his arms up and down so wildly that he fell off the branch and into some ferns, laughing loudly.

"Practice, practice, fledgling," pronounced the parrot and flew away.

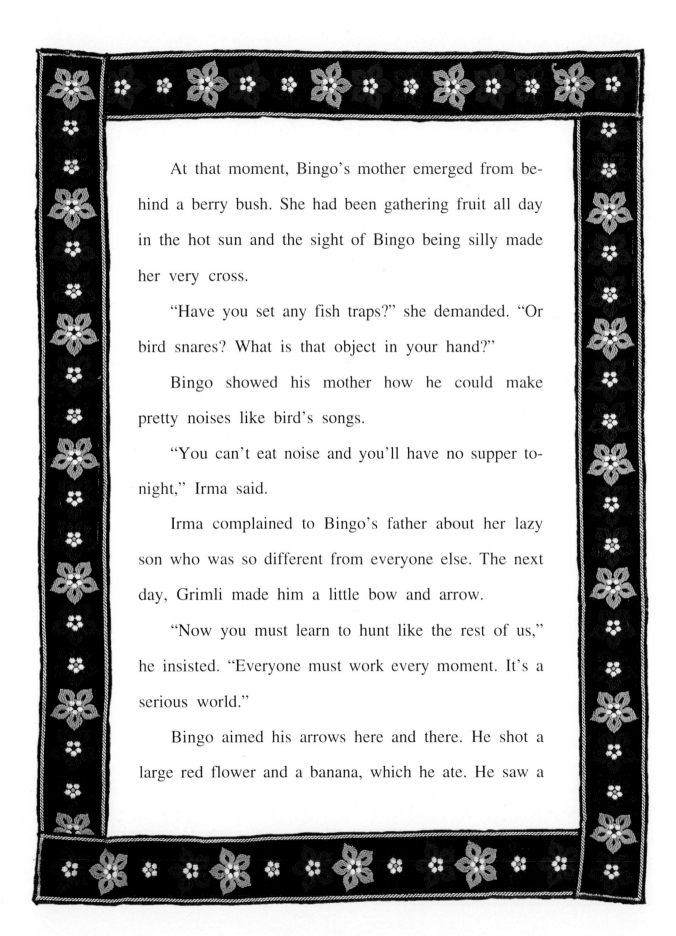

At that moment, Bingo's mother emerged from behind a berry bush. She had been gathering fruit all day in the hot sun and the sight of Bingo being silly made her very cross.

"Have you set any fish traps?" she demanded. "Or bird snares? What is that object in your hand?"

Bingo showed his mother how he could make pretty noises like bird's songs.

"You can't eat noise and you'll have no supper tonight," Irma said.

Irma complained to Bingo's father about her lazy son who was so different from everyone else. The next day, Grimli made him a little bow and arrow.

"Now you must learn to hunt like the rest of us," he insisted. "Everyone must work every moment. It's a serious world."

Bingo aimed his arrows here and there. He shot a large red flower and a banana, which he ate. He saw a big green lizard with popping eyes sitting on a rock and curling its tongue to catch bugs.

"Hello, Chameleon, are you good to eat?" said Bingo politely.

The chameleon said nothing and Bingo shot a mushroom. By that time he felt the need to rest, so he sat down under a shady tree. He idly poked his arrow into the dirt beside him. It made marks that somehow turned into a fish, and then he scratched some more and like magic a lizard appeared etched into the ground.

"Look," said Bingo, laughing excitedly and turning to the chameleon, "it's you!"

The chameleon rolled his eyes and blinked.

When Grimli came looking for him, Bingo couldn't wait to tell him. "There's a fish and there's a lizard, and I made them!"

Grimli was at first puzzled and then angry. "You

can't eat such a fish or lizard," he said. "You must learn to be like the others. Tomorrow you will spend all day tending the fire, and if it goes out . . ." He never said what he would do, but Bingo had a good imagination and he was very worried.

All the next morning, Bingo sat by the fire feeding the red flames with little twigs and blowing on the hot coals to make sure they were still alive. The sweat ran down his cheeks. His eyelids were heavy and his throat burned. He heard the sound of the nearby river swirling about the rocks. Surely he could go for a quick drink and come right back. Off he ran to the slippery banks of the stream and leaned over to catch some water in his hands. Before he could stop himself, he had fallen in.

"A-ah," said Bingo, for it felt so cool.

"O-oh," cried Bingo, for the fast current was pulling him downstream.

He wiggled his arms and splashed with his legs and surprisingly found himself traveling like a fish. How wonderful! Just in front of him, he saw a brown log floating and was just about to grab it when the log opened its mouth, showing sharp white teeth, and turned into a crocodile.

"No!" shouted Bingo, throwing up his arms, which made his feet go down and touch the sandy bottom. In a moment, he had scrambled up the bank and away from the crocodile, who was too sleepy to follow him.

"Catch-as-catch-can," shouted Bingo laughing merrily.

"You *are* caught," said a deep voice as a strong hand grabbed him. He looked up into Grimli's furious face. But Bingo, perhaps because he was wet and muddy, or because his fright gave him unexpected strength, escaped. He raced like an antelope through the forest, his heart thumping madly as he twisted and turned. The high ferns covered his small body until he came to a tiny cave just big enough for him. While entering it, he passed the very lizard whose image he had drawn in the dirt. He had only one breathless moment in which to hold a finger to his lips as he gazed into the lizard's round eyes, and then the darkness of the cave hid him.

Just then, Grimli came rushing up and saw the cave. He also saw a large chameleon sitting on a warm rock in front of it, lazily flicking its tongue.

"Have you seen my son?" roared Bingo's father. The lizard rolled his big eyes upward as if seeking an answer in the sky and shook his green head no.

Later that night, Bingo crept home through the forest carrying his friend the chameleon on his head. He was hungry, of course, but he was also very sorry.

Early the next morning, his angry father discovered him and the lizard asleep together and woke them up.

"Life is a serious business," said his father, drawing his eyebrows together. "There is no time for anything but work, but you make music and pictures and swim like a fish. Why do you do these strange things?"

Bingo stroked the chameleon softly and thought before he spoke. "Music and pictures are happy things. If we work *all* the time we have no time to hear the birds or see the beautiful moon and stars. We have no time to learn about all the wonderful things in the world. And," he added, "it's fun to laugh."

For a long time Bingo's father thought about these new things. He smoked his pipe and thought and stared at the lizard, who stared back at him with his great, round eyes.

Then he took out the moonstones from his pouch for the first time. "You are wise, my son," he finally declared. "We grown-ups should learn some very important things. From now on, the Efe will play music and make pictures in praise of life's goodness. And you," he said, staring back at the chameleon, "deserve a reward for being my son's protector. I will throw my magic stones for the first time. Bingo will someday be the leader, and I will give them to him to use in the future."

He threw the black stones and pronounced, "I will give you the power to change your color according to your surroundings. In this way, you will always be protected and can also amuse children."

From that long-ago time until today, the Efe Pygmies play music and make art in the Ituri Forest. Pygmy children still walk about with their pet chameleons on their heads, and when they put them down on bright flowers to watch them change color, they always smile.

THE QUARRELING
QUAIL

India

Not so very long ago in a cool green forest in India, there lived a large family of quail. There was a father quail who was generally thought of as the leader, except by his wife, and many children, aunts, uncles, and cousins. In fact, only a few of the young and impressionable birds thought of Father Quail as a leader. The rest of the flock were simply too lazy to take over his job.

They lived much the same lives as other quail, eating seeds and insects and sleeping in a circle, their heads facing outward, so that no enemy could approach unseen. This was a wise precaution, for unlike ordinary dull brown quail, these birds had feathers that were a fantastic mix of brilliant colors, feathers that a bird catcher, or fowler, could sell for a small fortune in the market square.

Father Quail, much to Mother Quail's annoyance, could not stop himself from looking into any pool of water that made a looking glass. Flashing his wings and tossing his head, he would repeat, "Even the peacocks in the Raja's palace garden are not so fine."

Mother Quail warned him sternly, "Don't forget your duty, sir! You are our guardian. Your whistle must warn of danger and save the covey."

For a few days, Father Quail would sit steadfastly on his high perch and whistle his long, clear note, calling the quail together to hide and save themselves when danger was near. Once they gathered to hide from a hawk and again from a fox, who slinked by as

they huddled in the tall grass, their hearts beating like tiny drums.

But soon Father Quail grew careless again. A nearby pond attracted his eye and he peered into it to see his dazzling reflection.

"Lilac, turquoise, blue, and gold," he murmured. "Feathers fit for a raja. Was there ever anything so handsome?"

"Fit for a raja, indeed!" snapped Mother Quail. "And what would you be wearing while his royal highness decorated his turban with your feathers?"

Father Quail shuddered and turned his golden brown eyes from side to side searching the undergrowth nervously for signs of a bird catcher and his net.

The other quail found him rather tiresome and vain. "We are all beautiful," they whispered to each other. "And most of us would do a much better job of protecting the covey."

But Father Quail could not keep his small mind completely on his job, and it was, sad to say, just as he stood once more gazing at himself in a little pool left by the rain that Manu, a poor fowler, wandered into the forest clearing where the quail lived. Father Quail raised his magnificently colored wings and watched them make rainbows in the water as he fluttered them up and down. Manu gasped in amazement, and that tiny sound saved Father Quail from the fowler's net. He arose in a blaze of color shrilling his warning note. The other birds, all but one uncle who was busy eating a particularly fat worm, quickly gathered and escaped.

"See what your vanity has done," the other quail angrily shrieked. "Uncle is gone!"

"Handsome is as handsome does," said Mother Quail severely.

Father Quail was so ashamed that when he saw a puddle he shut his golden brown eyes and bowed his head. He walked into its watery, muddy center and splashed his wings, stirring up the mud until his beautiful plumage was covered by it and he appeared as dull and brown as any ordinary quail.

Manu returned home with only one bird. His angry wife said she could not make a meal from this small catch, and his four children quarreled over the pretty quail feathers. All the next day, much to his family's annoyance, Manu practiced whistling just one note, the very same note that Father Quail sounded when he warned of danger. When Manu was sure that he could duplicate it exactly, he returned to the forest, net in hand. He crept through the underbrush as noiselessly as a snake until he came to the edge of the clearing. Pursing his lips, he whistled that one note as high and clear as the sound of a flute. The birds gathered, imagining that Father Quail was calling them, and Manu quickly caught several cousins and two old aunts under his net. He sold them for a good sum in the marketplace.

Father Quail was at first terribly ashamed and then very angry and sad at the same time. He looked down at his stiff, brown, and colorless feathers and thought how they reflected the way he felt. And then, suddenly, he imagined himself as he had been, as magnificent as a finely clothed noble at the palace, the Raja himself, perhaps, a man who had cast off his rich, gaudy raiment for a simple suit of armor in which to go to battle. *He* was that warrior and a changed bird. His beak lifted. A look of leadership transformed him, and a fiery light appeared in his eyes. Mother Quail observed this with much surprise and even pride as he called the remaining birds to him.

"Soon there will be no more of us," he warned. "We must have a plan. The next time that evil fowler comes, you must each poke your beaks through the opening in his net."

The birds twittered in horror. "Has he gone mad? It will be the death of us all."

"Never fear, birdlings," continued Father Quail. "When your heads are in the holes you must at once and together fly to the nearest thornbush. The net will catch on the thorns and you will be able to free yourselves and fly away."

The next day, Manu came once again to the forest. When they answered his whistle, he threw his net over them. This time the quail flew off to a nearby thornbush and tore off the net. They laughed merrily at their easy escape. How wise Father Quail had been, but they were also very clever and brave. Together they had won.

Manu retreated empty-handed. Again he faced an angry wife who had been looking forward to more money for the family. The children screamed and yelled at each other, for they too were unhappy, having lost their chance to buy sweets in the market. Manu observed them gloomily as he sipped his tea. But, as he watched them hitting each other and grabbing toys, his mood suddenly lightened. An idea had occurred to him.

The following day, net in hand, he took off into the forest and quietly found his way to the little clearing where he had found the quail before. On his way, he stopped from time to time to pick up pebbles, which he put into a small bag hanging from his sash.

Luckily, he found the large group of quail eating insects and seedlings. Instead of whistling, he hid himself and threw the pebbles one by one among the birds.

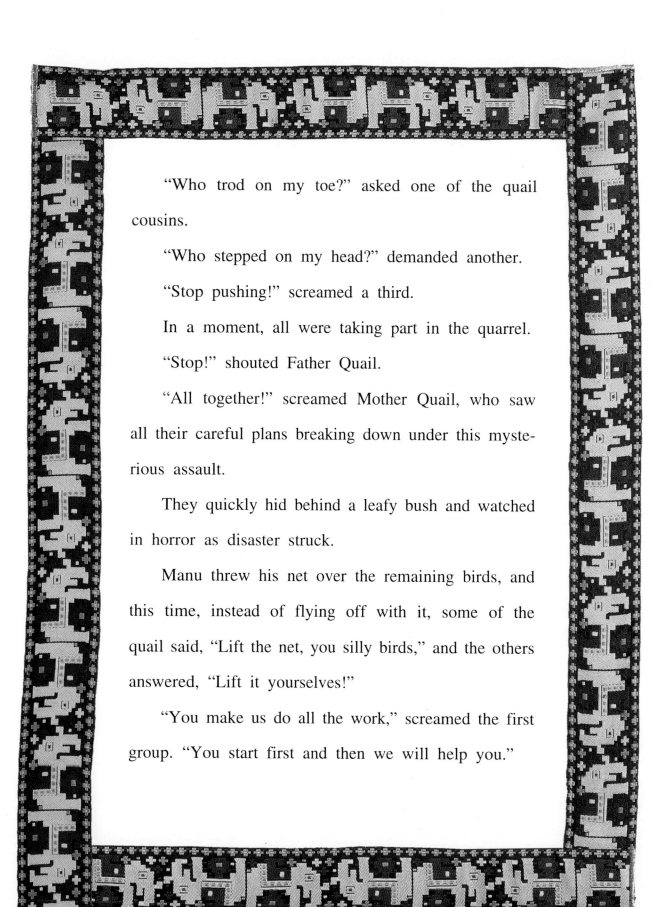

"Who trod on my toe?" asked one of the quail cousins.

"Who stepped on my head?" demanded another.

"Stop pushing!" screamed a third.

In a moment, all were taking part in the quarrel.

"Stop!" shouted Father Quail.

"All together!" screamed Mother Quail, who saw all their careful plans breaking down under this mysterious assault.

They quickly hid behind a leafy bush and watched in horror as disaster struck.

Manu threw his net over the remaining birds, and this time, instead of flying off with it, some of the quail said, "Lift the net, you silly birds," and the others answered, "Lift it yourselves!"

"You make us do all the work," screamed the first group. "You start first and then we will help you."

While they quarreled, the fowler easily gathered them up in his net and took them directly to the Raja's palace, where he sold the beautiful birds for a large sum. Some time later, a bedraggled Father and Mother Quail emerged from their hiding place. They were sad but glad to be alive. A gentle rain began to fall, and as the two birds huddled together, Father Quail's mud gradually melted and spread until Mother Quail was an ordinary bird too, a fit mate for her husband.

And so they stayed. Their glorious feathers hidden, they were no longer hunted and lived long and happy lives. As for Manu, when he finally reached home, his wife greeted him with a warm smile at his success, and his children were happy when their father bought them sweets and ices at the market.

"Because I got an idea from your quarreling, I was able to capture the quail and get the money for our treats," he said. "But now I must tell you a story so

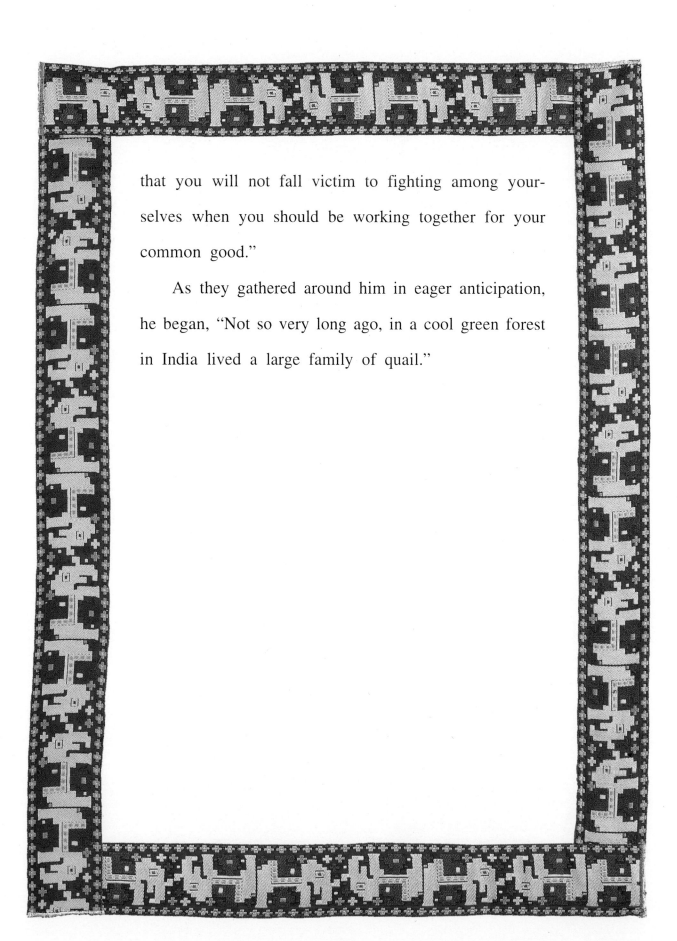

that you will not fall victim to fighting among yourselves when you should be working together for your
common good."

As they gathered around him in eager anticipation,
he began, "Not so very long ago, in a cool green forest
in India lived a large family of quail."

SISTER BEAR

Native American

One spring day, during the time of the strawberry moon, a young Indian girl called Little Bear lay fast asleep on a hillside shaded by the blue shadow of some pine trees. The pine needles were soft and her stomach was full of the berries she had been picking all morning. Her face was painted with red berry juice like war paint. She smiled, for in her sleep something cold and wet touched her cheek as if the last icicle of winter were melting away and dripping down on her. Then a curious snuffling sounded in her ear and a tickling feeling made her awaken suddenly. She sneezed and sat facing a small, brown cub who sat down abruptly on its round bottom and slid halfway down the hill on the slippery pine needles.

Little Bear was charmed. In an instant, she had slid down the slope too, whooping merrily. But as the noise of her laughter rang out, she covered her mouth with her hands to stifle it. In her mind, she heard Grandfather's voice telling her, "Watch out for Mother Bear. When her babies are about she will attack anything or anyone that might do them harm."

She looked around carefully, but the hilly slope was empty. The yellow butterflies quivered gently in the air and no bird sounded a warning.

"Have you lost your mother, small one?" inquired Little Bear kindly. The cub leaned forward in a rather anxious way and licked her hand.

"You are hungry, poor thing." The child went instantly to get her basket of strawberries, which she had placed under a bush.

As the little animal gobbled up the strawberries, staining its muzzle and paws, Little Bear smiled in delight. They looked so much alike! Both were round and brown and both had sparkling eyes and a taste for sweets.

"My name is Little Bear, so you can be my Sister Bear," said Little Bear conversationally. She had no sister and here was one ready-made and more fun than most.

They spent an hour or two sliding and watching to see where the honeybees went. Little Bear picked some dandelion greens to make a spring tea, as there were no more berries to be found. Then they strolled happily home and into her mother's tepee.

Little Bear's mother was not greatly pleased to see this newfound companion, but she was not altogether surprised. Her daughter was always bringing home friends, odd snakes, birds with broken wings, and injured rabbits. Once she had even arrived with a skunk, who had quickly outworn his welcome. All of them she had nursed to health, making compresses of plantain leaves for their cuts and sores and splints for their broken bones.

"And what is this?" her mother inquired, adding some more wood to her fire. "Our dinner? Or a fine fur coat to keep you warm when the first snow flies?"

"Oh, no. It is Sister Bear."

"And what does Sister Bear do?" asked her mother shrewdly. "Eat all our berries and steal our food? Indian girls must help gather nuts and grind corn for the winter and make moccasins."

Little Bear thought quickly, and at the same time it occurred to her that she didn't wish to do these things any more than Sister Bear would.

"Oh." She gulped. "We can go fishing and she can spear fish on her sharp claws. And she can find where

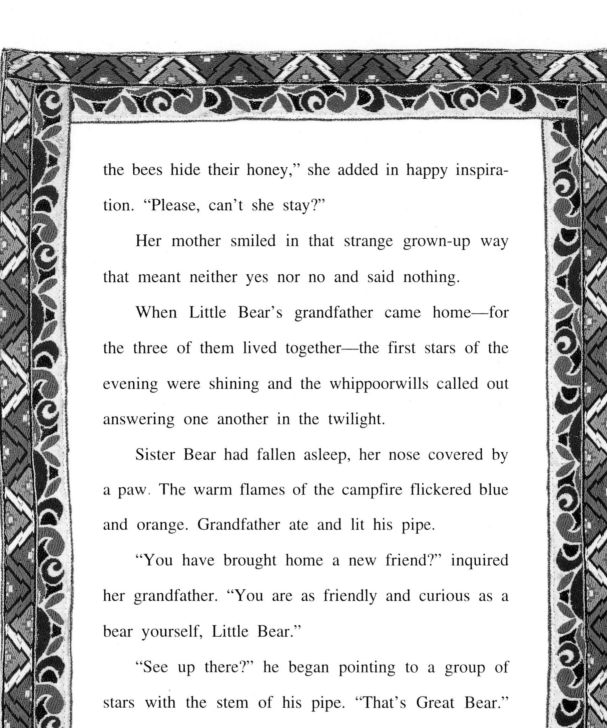

the bees hide their honey," she added in happy inspiration. "Please, can't she stay?"

Her mother smiled in that strange grown-up way that meant neither yes nor no and said nothing.

When Little Bear's grandfather came home—for the three of them lived together—the first stars of the evening were shining and the whippoorwills called out answering one another in the twilight.

Sister Bear had fallen asleep, her nose covered by a paw. The warm flames of the campfire flickered blue and orange. Grandfather ate and lit his pipe.

"You have brought home a new friend?" inquired her grandfather. "You are as friendly and curious as a bear yourself, Little Bear."

"See up there?" he began pointing to a group of stars with the stem of his pipe. "That's Great Bear." Little Bear leaned against his encircling arm, knowing that a story was about to be told. "And those stars here

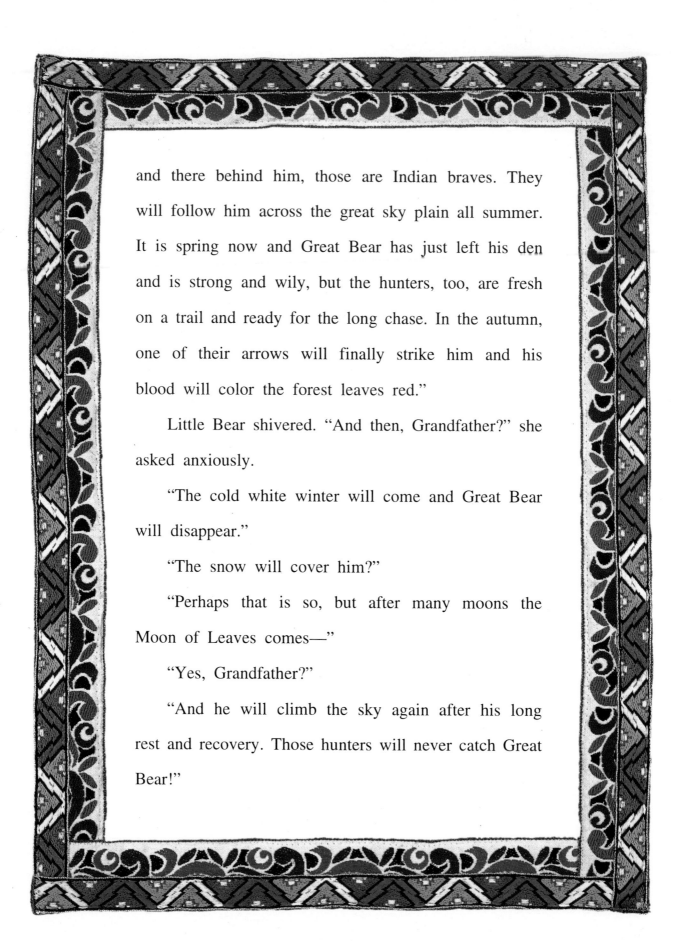

and there behind him, those are Indian braves. They will follow him across the great sky plain all summer. It is spring now and Great Bear has just left his den and is strong and wily, but the hunters, too, are fresh on a trail and ready for the long chase. In the autumn, one of their arrows will finally strike him and his blood will color the forest leaves red."

Little Bear shivered. "And then, Grandfather?" she asked anxiously.

"The cold white winter will come and Great Bear will disappear."

"The snow will cover him?"

"Perhaps that is so, but after many moons the Moon of Leaves comes—"

"Yes, Grandfather?"

"And he will climb the sky again after his long rest and recovery. Those hunters will never catch Great Bear!"

Little Bear smiled in relief. "This is Sister Bear's Moon of Leaves," she said. "Winter is a long, long time away."

She yawned, and as sleep made her eyes heavy, rolled over to curl up with Sister Bear for the night.

The next day, Little Bear and Sister Bear awoke to the early morning sun and found themselves surrounded by curious Indian children. Some of them had sticks and were prodding the sleepy cub. Sister Bear snarled and Little Bear yelled.

The children laughed, for they also saw how much alike the two were.

"You Bear girls," they shouted. "You belong to the Bear tribe and not the Indian people."

Little Bear's black brows drew together as she held Sister Bear close. "Well you," she said, glaring at a boy with a rather long, pointed nose and round eyes, "belong to the silly Goose tribe. And you," she added, picking out two girls screaming with hoarse shouts, "must be the tribe of Ismasques, the fish hawks."

In a moment, peals of laughter rang out as everyone thought of new and funnier tribal names for each other and for themselves. But from then on, Little Bear was called Girl Bear.

Moons came and went. The girls of the tribe gathered berries and dried them and shelled walnuts and pecans to be stored in rawhide cases for the cold winter. They ground maize and sewed deerskin into warm robes while the boys and men hunted.

Girl Bear and Sister Bear did not follow the traditional paths. They went fishing and caught painted trout. They tracked the bees and stole their honey. Sometimes the warrior bees, buzzing angrily, chased them through the forest, and they had to jump into the nearest water to hide beneath the surface and escape or plaster their stinging bites with mud. And Girl Bear always came back with rosehips and mint and raspberry leaves for tea, and leaves of trees and plants for healing the skin and soothing colds and sore throats.

Some of the Indian maidens, looking at Girl Bear's wild black hair decorated with brightly colored bird feathers and her scratched arms and legs, would smile contemptuously.

"What brave will ever choose Girl Bear?" whispered Moonflower.

"Maybe another bear will marry her," said Nohomis, giggling unkindly.

Girl Bear's mother heard the talk and thought to herself that it was time for Sister Bear to leave and for Girl Bear to become like the others.

"When the early snow comes, your friend must go," she announced one day, in a voice that asked for no answer but obedience.

It was but the beginning of the Harvest Moon and

Girl Bear thought, "It is early yet and moons to come. Who knows what may happen?"

One morning, the two friends awoke to a white crispness in the air and Girl Bear suddenly noticed the orange and red leaves against the blue sky. With a cold shiver she remember Grandfather's campfire story.

They walked slowly down to the lake and looked into the rippling water. A large bear stood reflected there, and beside it stood a tall Indian maiden. Girl Bear slid to the ground and put an arm around her furred friend's brown shoulders. She let out a great sigh. Sister Bear touched her cheek with her cold, black nose, just as she had when they had first met, and whined softly. Somehow, just as the seasons had changed, so had they. The carefree days of spring and the long, hurried days of summer had changed into a cold, grey season, and a few snowflakes sprinkled suddenly in the air.

That night the huge harvest moon hung over the tepees and the campfires sent long plumes of smoke toward the stars.

In the morning, Sister Bear was gone.

It was not long, and before the trail had grown cold, that Girl Bear followed. Her mother and grandfather hugged her warmly and sent her well laden with dried venison, the fruits of summer, and all her medicines.

"For you of the Bear clan are curious," said her mother. "Your path is a different one, my daughter. I hope, in its twists and turns, it will return you to us once again."

So Girl Bear followed the long trail to find her friend and herself. It began in a swirl of autumn leaves and ended in the deep white snows of winter. In the end, she discovered the small cave where Sister Bear lay deep asleep and settled down beside her to keep warm and safe.

Just what happened in those cold months when everything disappeared under a cover of white no one really knows. But when the Moon of Leaves shone once again in the sky, Indians told stories of a great bear with two cubs accompanied by a young woman who was believed to possess magical powers; for that is how she could travel safely in such company.

One day, after many seasons, Girl Bear came home, to the great joy of her mother and grandfather. Tall and brown, she carried with her many secrets and medicines of the wild and became known by the name that she carried the rest of her life, Wise Bear, the caretaker of all her tribe.

On full-moon nights, she sometimes has visitors from the Bear clan who are the chiefs of the council of animals. They leave footprints both large and small but are never seen. They come to talk to Wise Bear, it is said, for she is their friend.